Secret Places

LIVING OUT
Gay and Lesbian Autobiographies

Joan Larkin and David Bergman
GENERAL EDITORS

The Other Mother: A Lesbian's Fight for Her Daughter
Nancy Abrams

An Underground Life: Memoirs of a Gay Jew in Nazi Berlin
Gad Beck

Development and *Two Selves*
Bryher

The Hurry-Up Song: A Memoir of Losing My Brother
Clifford Chase

In My Father's Arms: A True Story of Incest
Walter A. de Milly III

Midlife Queer: Autobiography of a Decade, 1971–1981
Martin Duberman

Widescreen Dreams: Growing Up Gay at the Movies
Patrick E. Horrigan

Eminent Maricones: Arenas, Lorca, Puig, and Me
Jaime Manrique

Taboo
Boyer Rickel

Secret Places: My Life in New York and New Guinea
Tobias Schneebaum

Secret Places

MY LIFE IN NEW YORK AND NEW GUINEA

Tobias Schneebaum

The University of Wisconsin Press

The University of Wisconsin Press
2537 Daniels Street
Madison, Wisconsin 53718

3 Henrietta Street
London WC2E 8LU, England

1   3   5   4   2

Printed in the United States of America

Library of Congress Cataloging-in-Publication Data
Schneebaum, Tobias.
Secret places: my life in New York
and New Guinea / Tobias Schneebaum.
184 pp.   cm. — (Living out)
ISBN 0-299-16990-1 (cloth: alk. paper)
1. Schneebaum, Tobias.
2. Ethnologists—United States—Biography.
3. Gay men—United States—Biography.
4. Asmat (Indonesian people) I. Title. II. Series.
GN21.S287 A3   2000
305.8′0092—dc21   00-008602

for Floriano Vecchi
Allan Gurganus
Rick Whitaker

We who dwell on Earth can do nothing of ourselves,
every thing is conducted by Spirits.
                                    —William Blake, *Jerusalem*

Contents

Illustrations

Foreword

A Taste of Tobias Schneebaum

David Bergman

When I first met Tobias Schneebaum, he was holding a phallus that was a good foot and a half long. "It arrived today. Isn't it marvelous!" he announced proudly and placed it in the middle of the dining table for all of us to admire. We were at the apartment of the poet Edward Field and Field's novelist companion of thirty years, Neil Derrick. They had invited Schneebaum to dinner as a surprise for me, since I had told them how much I wanted to meet him. Neil, who is blind, picked up the phallus to feel it. "Yes, quite marvelous!" he confirmed, smiling.

It took a while for Tobias to take his eyes off his latest acquisition, which gave me the chance to look him over. He wasn't what I expected of a man who had spent his life among headhunters and cannibals. He looked like my late Uncle Moe, an economist and amateur Talmudic scholar. In his mid-seventies, Schneebaum was small, bent, and sallow, with a large nose that seemed slightly red. A cold? Drink? Or, as it turned out to be, the result of years of living near the equator. Eventually, Tobias turned to me with his large, watery eyes and said, "I thought you'd like to see it. I couldn't bring it back from New Guinea in my luggage—it was too heavy—so I asked a young couple if they would mail it when they got to the States, and here it is!" The phallus drooped a bit; it was made of a ropy fiber wrapped with what looked like electrical tape, but was probably bark. Only the head was hard, and it bulged like an unripe plum.

He had just taken a group of tourists to an island in West Papua in Indonesian New Guinea where they had witnessed the ceremonial dance in which each of the men wore one of the phalluses. "What's that bobbing between the men's legs?" the visitors had asked Schneebaum. "Penises," he answered, and they all turned away. "I don't understand them," Schneebaum commented, his head shaking, "they've come thousands of miles to see something they would never see in New Rochelle, and when you show it to them, they turn their backs." Only now do I realize that the incident had been something of a test for me, a challenge. Would I be shocked? Would I turn away? Or would I—as Schneebaum had throughout his life— regard this art of a different world with delight and appreciation.

For Schneebaum is a man who regards life as a series of initiations, and, as any anthropologist will tell you, initiations are complicated affairs. They are not merely tests of endurance and sympathy, or introductions into tribal mysteries, but primarily inductions into communities. They isolate you as a way of preparing you for inclusion. They bind you to others even as they separate you from everyone. Schneebaum has always oscillated between his competing needs for communal acceptance and personal independence, between the desire for individuality and anonymity, between being possessed by others and self-realization.

This fundamental tension in his personality seems to have emerged quite early in his life. In some ways, he is the classic middle child, enjoying neither the privileges of being first nor the advantages of being last. As a boy, he could choose either to fade out of sight or to fight for recognition. Moreover, he suffered under what he then felt was the rule of a father "obsessed with religion and discipline . . . and full of cruelty," a regime that made him want by turns to disappear and to rebel.* Today Schneebaum cannot judge just how violent his father was, yet he knows that he was the particular target of his wrath. More than once, he's asked himself: "Did my father seek me out to punish me? Or did I seek the punishment" (*Wild Man*, 6)? Did he search out the spotlight like an actor? Or did he have it turned on him like a prisoner trying to escape? Has he sought the most remote areas of the world to get lost or to gain attention? No wonder Schneebaum has sought both identification with and love from the Wild Man—that archetype of outward violence and inner love, of unrestrained action and tribal attachment—since the figure of the Wild Man merges both him and his father. For his father, whom Schneebaum

---

*Tobias Schneebaum, *Wild Man* (New York: Viking, 1979), 4. [Cited hereafter in the text as *Wild Man*]

cannot forgive for violence, on whose death he claims to have "felt nothing," was the first of many Wild Men whom Schneebaum hoped to seduce and incorporate, "the one that I would love"*(*Wild Man,* 2). His father initiated him into rituals that Schneebaum has spent his life performing, rituals that combine violence and affection, hardship and joyousness, cruelty and community.

Rituals, anthropologists tell us, painstakingly create boundaries, only to invite their transgression. They are processes of both isolation and assimilation. Schneebaum's father performed just such rituals. For example, although he never smiled at his family or "showed a single sign of affection," the elder Schneebaum would "weep in sympathy with the characters" in the stories printed in the *Jewish Daily Forward* (*Wild Man,* 4). After his father left (no doubt under provocation) his home in eastern Poland to come to the United States, he never returned. And when he set up shop in Brooklyn as a grocer, he selected a store not in a Jewish neighborhood, but in a Scandinavian one. For all his parochial insularity, his father was a man who chose to be in strange company and make concessions to foreign ways. Schneebaum's mother also contributed to his respect for ritual boundaries and the compulsion to transgress them. Before her marriage, she worked as a janitor for a row of tenements in the Lower East Side, carrying out cans of garbage, heavy man's work. But when it came time to marry, she followed the traditional route, consulting the local *shadchan,* who arranged it. She was the one who made sure that the rabbi came to teach Talmud to Tobias and his brothers, and it is from her that he gained his mysticism.

Schneebaum's decision to study art, made when in high school, was another act of love and rebellion. He went against his father's wishes by taking classes in life drawing, and had to hide his sketches because his father disapproved of nudity. Even going to City College, where he majored in math, was an act of rebellion, since his father wanted him to quit school and work full time in his grocery. Yet studying both art and mathematics subjected Schneebaum to a discipline as severe as, if less harsh than, his father's, and while they separated Tobias from his family, they involved him in a larger community. They were his own form of separation and assimilation.

Being a Jew both singled him out and connected him to communities. As a soldier assigned to Baer Field in Fort Wayne, Indiana, he encountered an anti-Semitism so unquestioning of its propriety that it did not even think to disguise itself. In Alaska as a civilian, he was told to "go back to where [he] came from" because he was a Jew (*Wild Man,* 21). But when Schneebaum was a boy, Judaism hadn't supplied him with a source of belonging. When he studied for his bar mitzvah, that rite of passage into

adulthood, the rabbi "never gave any indication of approval and often clumped [him] painfully on the head for any wrong vowel sound, and when he did so, crumbs fell from his beard on to the pages of the book." *
The crumbs are a wonderful detail, suggesting the boorish hunger of the man, his uncontrollable appetite, which literally spills over into his learning, and the almost suffocating closeness of his training. Years later, Schneebaum would recall those moments with a new appreciation. During his initiation into an Asmat community, when "the men and the forest forced their presence into [him]," the image of the rabbi returned, and he understood that "the child sitting next to Rabbi [is] the same me who stood next to a naked black warrior, his nose stuffed with spiraling shells, his face painted white" (*Spirits*, 43). The reverse proved true as well. At a Hasidic wedding, Schneebaum felt "the same joy that I felt as I watched and listened to the chanting monks in Burma" (*Wild Man*, 154). But this recognition that Judaism contains a similar wildness and community dawned on Schneebaum only after many decades of travel. As a young man, he could see "nothing of the wild rejoicing of the Hasidim" (*Wild Man*, 155).

Schneebaum did not start off as a world traveler. As a youth, his travels were limited to New York City, and as a radar mechanic, he was stationed in the United States. Only after World War II did he travel abroad, and then to a rather conventional destination, one close to home—Mexico. The trip was inspired by the painter and muralist Rufino Tamayo, with whom Schneebaum studied soon after returning to civilian life. In Mexico, Schneebaum glimpsed for the first time people untouched by Western ways. The Lacandón, who had lived unnoticed in the rain forests of the Yucatán, had been discovered only three years before Schneebaum visited them. They still hunted with bows and arrows, and followed their own ways. Brief as Schneebaum's exposure was, the Lacandón transported him back in time and out of his own body. The trip to Mexico was memorable for another reason: for the first time, he found himself involved in a circle of gay men, artists and friends, whose passions and intrigues swirled around him. Schneebaum had refrained from sex after some adolescent experiences; now in the Mexican town of Ajijic, his homosexual desires were reawakened.

Schneebaum's trip to Mexico began a pattern that he would follow for several decades. He would work for several months for Tiber Press, a greeting-card company. With the money he earned, he traveled during the rest of the year. Not that Schneebaum earned much, even when his

*Tobias Schneebaum, *Where the Spirits Dwell: An Odyssey in the Jungles of New Guinea* (New York: Grove Press, 1988), 13. [Cited hereafter in the text as *Spirits*]

earnings at Tiber Press were supplemented with the sales of paintings. His travels were made possible because the dollar was strong and he traveled as cheaply as possible. He often walked because it was the only way to get to where he wanted. He used tramp steamers and canoes. He slept in seedy hotels, in barns and tents, beside the road, and under the stars. In one of Schneebaum's closest encounters with death, he hitched a ride on a truck going through the Sahara from Sebha in central Libya to Faya Largeau in northern Chad. Without roads through the desert, the drivers navigated by instinct. Three days out of Sebha—not having encountered another person—the truck broke its rear axle, and Schneebaum knew that it might be weeks before anyone passed them or just as long for someone in their group to return from the nearest village with help. Their rations of water would not sustain them. They were as good as dead:

Suddenly [the driver and his crew] got up, climbed onto the truck, and began unloading. Everything came down—boxes, crates, firewood, barrels, drums, goods, tools, spare parts for the truck, water, gasoline. When it got dark, we had supper and went to sleep. In the morning, after prayers, the unloading continued. Chari [the driver] let out a yell and pushed an iron bar down from the truck. It had been at the very bottom, a spare part almost forgotten. No one had thought there would be a use for it. Carefully, the rust was scraped off the bar with sand. The truck jacked up, the broken axle removed, and I was asked to examine the serial numbers. Miraculously, they matched. That night we rejoiced when the truck again began to move, and in the morning we loaded up the mass of goods. (*Wild Man*, 182)

No four-star hotels for Schneebaum, no help from American Express. Schneebaum again and again relies on the kindness of strangers.

In 1956, his life changed. Schneebaum won a Fulbright Fellowship to study art in Peru, which allowed him to travel to the jungles on the extreme eastern border, where the Andes give way to the Amazon basin. Schneebaum was gone so long that the American Embassy concluded that he was dead, and reports of his death appeared in the Peruvian newspapers. But, as in the case of Mark Twain, such announcements were premature. The seven months, in which he was given up for dead, had been spent with the Akarama, a tribe of cannibals who had adopted him. For more than half a year, he had lived in a way that stretched back to a time before Columbus, to a time probably before the Aztecs had constructed their great empire.

Schneebaum tells the story of his life among the Akarama in his first book, *Keep the River on Your Right*, a book so tensely plotted, so exquisitely balanced, so lyrically written that it has been mistaken for a novel. Joseph Conrad's *Heart of Darkness* lurks behind it. Like Conrad's Marlow,

Schneebaum isn't merely transported directly into the lives of the indigenous people; he first moves through various levels of colonization. And like *Heart of Darkness, Keep the River on Your Right* explores the relationship between eros and thanatos; indeed, Schneebaum is motivated by the twin drives of love and death.

After leaving Lima, Schneebaum stays at a missionary outpost at the edge of the Amazon, manned by a colorful cast of characters. There is Father Moiseis, the kindly if somewhat sleepy priest, who has grown lax in his treatment of the indigenous people. He is attended by his faithful, puritanical, and humpbacked servant Hermano. And finally there is the dashingly handsome Manolo, a lay missionary, a cynical romantic and idealist, who, disillusioned with religion and love, has become the town whore, willing to go with any Indian who is "looking for a quick roll in the jungle with the great big white man."* Schneebaum hangs around the mission, learning the people's stories, helping with the medicine, but unable to make future plans until Wassen, a wizened elder, wanders into the compound because his entire village has been destroyed by the Akarama in one of their lightning raids. One look at Wassen is all that Schneebaum needs to realize "that out there in the forest were other people more primitive, other jungles wilder, other worlds that existed that needed my eyes to look at them" (*River*, 50).

Once out in the jungle, Schneebaum encounters the elusive Akarama, who miraculously adopt him, instead of eating him—their usual way of treating strangers. Being an Akarama, Schneebaum finds, has both its ups and its downs. Among the benefits is the uninhibited sexuality and companionship of the men's lodge, where the Akarama warriors sleep in a pile of twisted bodies. For the first time in his life, Schneebaum finds himself one of the gang, a fully accepted member of the tribe, and his sexual desires, rather than separating him from the other men, serve to unite him. He rejoices in the unconditional brotherhood in which he finds himself. The drawback of Akarama culture, for Schneebaum, is its indifference to individual human life. At first, this indifference seems only peculiar, as when Michii gives "no sign of pride or pleasure" at becoming a father, although the "mother and child were no more than ten feet away" (*River*, 86). Later, this indifference becomes more difficult to bear because it underpins the Akarama's cannibalism. Schneebaum realizes, even as he is carried away by the primal violence of their raid on innocent people, that the very impulse leaves him feeling empty, rather than satisfied, lost rather than contented, denied rather than affirmed. Schneebaum can make that

---

*Tobias Schneebaum, *Keep the River on Your Right* (New York: Grove Press, 1969), 56. [Cited hereafter in the text as *River*]

judgment not because he has stood back from the experience, but because he is so deeply implicated in it:

> We three were alone until Ilhuene, Baaldore and Reindude were in front of us. Reindude, cupping in his hand the heart from the being we had carried from so far away, the heart of he who had lived in the hut we had entered to kill. We stretched out flat on the ground, lined up, our shoulders touching. Michii looked up at the moon and showed it to the heart. He bit into it as if it were an apple, taking a large bite, almost half the heart, and chewed down several times, spit it into a hand, separated the meat into six sections and placed some into the mouths of each of us. We chewed and swallowed. He did the same with the other half of the heart. He turned Darinimbiak onto his stomach, lifted his hips so that he crouched on all fours. Darinimbiak growled, Mayaarii-há!. Michii growled, Mayaarii-há! bent down to lay himself upon Darinimbiak's back and entered him. (*River*, 107)

Unlike the tribesmen, who rejoice in their head-hunting because they believe it is necessary for the survival of their tribe, Schneebaum cannot share the exultation.

Cannibal communion and sexual congress are here not merely as metaphors for each other, as they are in Sylvia Plath's "Daddy," in which her father bites her "pretty red heart in two"; in this moment, they are quite literally linked together: the enemy's heart is an aphrodisiac that leads to a bestial coupling that, although not rape, is not entirely voluntary. After the raid, Schneebaum moves away from the Akarama. The final break occurs when Darinimbiak, the native with whom Schneebaum has fallen in love, sickens from dysentery. Despite all of Schneebaum's efforts, including returning with Darinimbiak to the mission for medicine, Darinimbiak dies. His fellow warriors will not mourn Darinimbiak. His life—any individual life—is not important to them. Their one concern is the survival of the tribe. Schneebaum comes to recognize that a culture that cannot mourn cannot love and that all the acceptance he has found, unconditional as it may have been, lacks the one thing he most values—the capacity to be loved for himself alone.

Schneebaum returned to the United States, but he did not stop traveling. His experience in Peru among the Akarama only whetted his appetite for sharing the quickened impulses of people uninhibited by Western values and for risking his life in the pursuit of sights no Westerner has seen.

We can measure exactly how foolhardy Schneebaum can be in his pursuit of the remote and the untouched by his trip to Nias, an island off the coast of Sumatra. What made the trip to Nias dangerous was not that Schneebaum visited the island when he was nearly fifty, but that he underwent the grueling trip while he was still recuperating from cancer surgery. Getting to Nias is so difficult that most of us would not have even attempted it. But Schneebaum made it especially difficult. First he traveled from New York to Los Angeles on a bus (that would have ended the trip for me); then he spent weeks on a Norwegian freighter where he reread *Middlemarch* (another gauge of his gluttony for punishment); and finally he sailed on the *Gunung Kawi,* a sixty-foot-long vessel, loaded with textiles and food and nearly a hundred passengers, in which he slept on a board "covered with a straw mat infested with roaches" (*Wild Man,* 164). When Schneebaum arrives in Gunungsitoli, the major town in Nias, he almost immediately arranges to go to Gomo, which is near La Husa, an ancient ceremonial site of massive carved rocks. Gomo is a hamlet so remote that it rarely had been visited by Westerners. Few of the area's indigenous people had even been to Gomo, and the route that Schneebaum chooses, over the objections of all his advisers, is through the high mountains, a journey that no European had ever managed on foot. Schneebaum refuses to worry. His guide, Ama Rudina, claims that Gomo is only eight miles away. It turns out to be twenty, and on the journey, Schneebaum's adhesions become painful. He grows dehydrated. Through an extraordinary act of will, Schneebaum eventually gets to Gomo, weak, delirious, and in pain, more dead than alive. But after resting in Gomo, he eventually manages to see La Husa, which proves to be a disappointment.

The trip to Gomo came at a crucial point in Schneebaum's career—a year after the publication of *Keep the River on Your Right.* In some way, the trip was meant to put the Akarama behind him, for his life among them had haunted him ever since he had left Peru, more than a dozen years before. But writing *Keep the River on Your Right* revived those memories rather than putting them to rest. The book is structured as a journal addressed to an unidentified friend, but actually it was written ten years after the experience. One has the sense that the events are happening right in front of Schneebaum. This intense vividness testifies to how fresh the episodes were in Schneebaum's mind. But why did it take Schneebaum a decade to write the book? One reason is that he did not consider himself a writer. He was a painter. He turned to writing only because the experience would not leave him. Second, he needed the time to make sense of his sojourn among the Akarama. So in 1968, while America roiled in political turmoil over the Vietnam War and civil rights, Schneebaum went off to Italy and let loose in three months the words that would make him much more famous as a writer than as an artist. Grove Press took the book almost immediately. It had been recommended by John Rechy, whose *City of Night,* a landmark of gay literature, had been an enormous success. Fittingly, *Keep the River on Your Right* was published in 1969, the year of the Stonewall riots. Its themes of sexual liberation and communal life perfectly fitted their times. But having become the author of *Keep the River on Your Right,* Schneebaum must have felt the need to go on, to test his limits in some new way, to put behind him the diminishment that comes after having completed any major work. For works like *Keep the River on Your Right* come directly out of a writer, leaving an enormous gap that must be either filled or bridged.

Since writing *Keep the River on Your Right,* Schneebaum has come out with a new book at a rate of one a decade. Each one goes over some of the same material, but they are all structured differently. The tightly plotted *Keep the River on Your Right,* with its climax and denouement, was followed by the picaresque *Wild Man. Where the Spirits Dwell* is baggier still, as concerned with ethnographic information as it is with Schneebaum's life among the Asmat. *Secret Places* is composed of discrete essays. With each volume, Schneebaum has found structures that are increasingly decentered: no single event is climactic, a point that the rest of action moves toward or away from. The destination is no longer the focus of his work; it is the journey itself. Schneebaum has passed the crisis that the publication of *Keep the River on Your Right* generated. The essay structure allows him, in the light of his new experiences, to form his past in an infinite number of ways.

Nevertheless, in the late 1960s, Schneebaum could not stop searching for what he recognized might be his "doom." No sooner did he hear of Michael Rockefeller's death, presumably at the hands of the Asmat, than Schneebaum yearned to travel to New Guinea, where, like some latter-day Walter Pater, he "would live out a life of heightened sensations," which for Schneebaum means "making friends, enemies, lovers, repressing nothing, carrying out my instincts to their natural completion" (*Wild Man,* 197). Stepping off the little prop plane that took him to Agats in Irian Jaya, he is immediately bewitched by the place and the people who clustered in curiosity around him:

My breathing was uncontrolled and a pain in my chest sent spasms through me, for I was suddenly looking at untamed savages with greased, shining, ringleted hair studded with black and white feathers, with teeth of wild boar flashing white against black skin as they curved through noses, with breastplates of a thousand tiny cowries hanging on their chests like dickies, and most striking of all, their long, thin gourd-covered penises erect, sticking up eight, twelve, twenty inches. . . . I stood there wanting to enter [their] circle, to fit into the mass, to be a molecule building the structure of their being; it was all I wanted, all I ever wanted. (*Wild Man,* 199)

Some readers have found in such passages suggestions of racism—a romanticism that positions the Asmat as some erotic Other that w ll free the White Man from his burden. Romantic this passage cert in' I wonder if the clinically detached ethnology is any less romantic, both in its claims of objectivity and in its avoidance of the taint of power. For the anthropologist who *merely* observes presupposes a distance that is the hallmark of authority. The very objectivity that she or he claims is itself an imposition of cultural values. And does anyone really subject him- or herself to the ordeal of anthropological fieldwork from scientific interest alone? I have never met an anthropologist who wasn't motivated by some deeper desire, all the more corrosive for being unacknowledged. Schneebaum comes to the Asmat for personal needs that he does not try to disguise, and it is his willingness to show his personal needs, his own vulnerability, that balances the inevitable privilege of his position. But it is not the exotic that attracts him; it is the familiar that drives him on. For the Asmat, as for the Akarama, Schneebaum feels unaccountable kinship, as though they were the long-lost tribes of Israel. Entering the Asmat world, seeing things from an Asmat perspective is not an effort for Schneebaum; it requires only dropping the veil from his eyes, seeing as he would himself see. One may fault Schneebaum for being an innocent, and he certainly is child-like. But it is his child-like innocence that makes it possible for him to enter these various cultures and communities, to be adopted into so many tribes, to gain acceptance from peoples who usually regard outsiders as dangerous and deadly. If Schneebaum has since gained the academic training of an anthropologist, he came to it from a very different route than most academics. His fieldwork came *before* his training; indeed his training came about as a way to preserve the very culture that he saw endangered by contact with the outside world. This book speaks eloquently against those who view the Asmat as obstacles in their exploitation of such valuable commodities as wood and oil or as exotics who might entertain the jaded tastes of certain Westerners.

At a time when most people are looking toward retirement, Schneebaum began a new apprenticeship. The missionaries in Agats had begun creating a museum of Asmat art; they needed someone to catalog the collection, acquire missing pieces, and inspire people to preserve their traditions. Schneebaum returned to the United States to learn how to organize such a collection, and for the last twenty years he devoted himself to organizing, understanding and preserving what he could of Asmat culture and arts. Now nearly eighty, and suffering from Parkinson's disease, he still is traveling—to New Guinea and, for the first time in forty years, back to Peru, where he found, to his amazement, a few of the men he wrote about in *Keep the River on Your Right* still alive.

We talked in his large studio, a single room, at once austere and filled to overflowing. A jungle of house plants cover the windows that look out toward the Hudson and the abandoned piers where gay men used to cruise like hunters in the forest. The gay village life of the 1970s is now as past as the head-hunting days of the Asmat. The crumbling Westside Highway has been torn down, and a duller, if safer, ordinary road has taken its place. But from where I sit, the river still glistens on his right. Books are everywhere, scattered on tables, piled on the floor. On the walls, hang rows of war shields, in the three basic styles Schneebaum identified. "But they're all big penises," Schneebaum points out, "if you look at the outline of the shields, although most anthropologists like to deny it." On one of my visits he fumed against a major museum that forced him to alter his slides. He was giving a lecture on the penis inserts some men of South Asia stick horizontally through the body of their foreskins, a variation of the Prince Albert. His slides showed them in use. The museum officials wanted him to reshoot the objects against velvet backgrounds, as if they were crude collar bars at Tiffany's, the curators afraid that the sight of so much genitalia would risk their government funding. "People say they want to see things, and then when its shown them, they turn their backs." Schneebaum's contempt is raw.

He rocks restlessly. Behind him are a dozen skulls, decorated with little shells and seeds.

"What are these?" I ask him.

"My ancestors," he answers. "when I'm adopted into a family, I'm usually given the head of an ancestor."

He goes to the shelf and picks one up as if he were Hamlet rediscovering Yorick. He puts it back. "They're all family except this one. He was an enemy. See," he says, showing me a neat thin hole bored through the cranium. "That's where they sucked the brains out."

Acknowledgments

There are several people I must thank for their encouragement and for their insights. They continue to believe in me and in my work, and for that I am grateful. This book has been through many transformations. I particularly want to thank Claire Brook, Joe Caldwell, the always faithful reader Berenice Cortelle, Douglas Newton, Steven Watson, and Douglas Wright. I also take this opportunity to thank my New York agent, Don Congdon, who supported my work through thick and thin. I thank, too, Tom Maschler, of Jonathan Cape in London, who sought me out in Asmat, and I thank Octavia of Abner Stein, also in London. Once again, I thank the Corporation of Yaddo for the residences that have helped me enormously. I must also thank those Crosiers I knew in Asmat, and, of course, I thank the Asmat people themselves for being so generous and so fascinating. Finally, I must thank my family in the Great Neck area who have helped me more than they will ever know.

Secret Places

Introduction

Asmat bewitches me.

I often feel possessed there, but what it is that possesses me is unclear. The forest churns up my insides when I am in the midst of immense trees in soggy soil, vines, and plant life that exude odors of decay. The forest continually draws me into conjuring up dreams of living naked, hunting wild boar and cassowary, birds and possum, and spending days in blinds awaiting whatever animal would come, killing it, skinning it, roasting it, eating it.

At times when traveling with no one but my paddlers, I sit in the canoe or lie down on my pandanus mat in the men's house and allow my mind to wander at will. I am impressionable: I am a million miles or more away. I am on some star of Orion or perhaps it is Sirius, brightest of them all. Perhaps I become one of the daughters of Atlas in the cluster of the Pleiades, or I am in some distant nebula, hurling myself headlong into the Void, through the night sky, a meteorite of myself landing easily on a star.

Throughout my life, I have been searching for a way to connect with other human beings. Suddenly, I find myself in a forest among the Asmat, living in their world of spirits, where I lose my insecurities and am content.

What brought me to this stage in the history of my life? Where did I go right? How did I finally choose a path out of oblivion, the path itself so marvelous to behold? I would not change that path even if it were possible to do so. I cling to the myth of my father's anger, for I almost willed him to be difficult.

I suppose that during my childhood he was angry and exasperated when he called out and I failed to come instantly. When I was drawing at the kitchen table, I would brook no interruption, or so I said to myself. I was frightened of my father and always ended up doing whatever it was that he wanted. I kept myself safe in a world of my own. I was obsessed with drawing and with my need to lose myself, willing myself into another world where my father could not wallop me. There was a time, for most of my life, in fact, when I thought him cruel, but now I see that he was only following a path created by his own father in Poland and maybe by his father's father.

How is it that my different worlds came together in Asmat? It has taken my entire life to reach this point. Oh, I have done wonders for myself with my drawings, winning a Hallmark prize when I was sixteen for some drawing or watercolor influenced by the work of Rouault, bold with figures outlined in black. Later, I tried to emulate my older brother, Moe, to follow in his footsteps, taking courses in higher mathematics at City College in New York. I liked the subject, but it was not for me. My brain could not absorb the material in a month that he could absorb in a day.

My younger brother, Bernie, had spent most of his army time in India, for which he developed a distaste. "Too much poverty," he said. I was a radar mechanic during World War II, mostly at Baer Field in Fort Wayne, Indiana. But I also spent time in other states, dismantling radar equipment.

A surprising confrontation came up one day when I went to the tool crib at Baer Field to check out some tubes. The WAAC who worked there looked at me and said, "That is a funny name you have. What is it? Where are you from?" Her hair was bleached blond, but it was badly in need of touching up. I looked back at her and smiled and said, with a face as straight as possible, "Oh, the name is German. It means 'tree of snow or snowtree.' My parents came from Poland. We are Jewish, you know." She stepped back and cried out, "Jewish! But I liked you!" Later, I heard her asking someone, "But where are his horns?!" "Horns?" I asked myself. Are there really people who still believe that Jews have horns like Michelangelo's statue of Moses in the church of St. Peter in Chains? It was my first encounter with real hatred.

I did nothing to distinguish myself during the war. I checked the instruments on board the C-47s that came in with machine-gun bullet holes in them and made sure the planes left in good repair. An occasional B-29 would come in, not an easy plane on which to work. It meant squeezing through the cabin to get to the equipment.

After the war, I plodded along, studying painting with Rufino Tamayo at night in the Brooklyn Museum while working in my father's grocery store during the day. I had made a deal with my father that I would work for him for two years and save as much money as I could. Then I would go by ship to France and live in Paris, studying and painting for however long my money lasted. Tamayo did not approve of my going to Paris: "There is nothing there now, no art, no food, nothing. Why don't you go to Mexico?" It did not take him long to convince me.

I took a bus from New York down to Mexico City, a trip of five days and five nights. Even in those younger days of mine, it was not an easy journey, but I enjoyed the whole of it. I had only one introduction, a handwritten note to the Arenal family, to be found at Paris Siete, a pension that took its name from the name of the street itself, where I might stay if the rooms were reasonably priced. It turned out to be just right for me, but I was asked to sign the register only after a rather lengthy interview about politics, which included asking for whom I had voted in the last election. Fortunately for my stay there, I had voted for Henry Wallace that year of 1948 and was welcomed into the pension.

Mexico City was marvelous in those days. In many ways, it must still be the same. I went to the Belles Artes almost every evening for dance performances, opera, or theater, all interesting and sometimes great. I would hesitate to go back to Mexico City now, with its frightening pollution. I had a very pleasant large room in the pension, which was on the same block as the Maria Christina Hotel, across from the Reforma Hotel. Paris Siete had an ornate façade on the outside and a mysterious atmosphere inside that I never understood. Some weeks after I moved in, I began noticing that closed-door meetings were being held there after supper every Wednesday. I had no idea what the meetings were about, but I did see David Siqueiros there a couple of times with his wife, one of the Arenal daughters. I met Frida Khalo and enjoyed my one-minute conversation with her. She was startlingly beautiful and weird. Of course, I decided that the meetings were being held in the name of the Communist Party. I may have met Carlos Merida there. No, that cannot be. Perhaps it was at the home of Annette Nancarrow. Impossible! Neither Carlos nor Annette was ever involved in the Party in any way.

It wasn't long before I met the Romanian woman who lived on the roof of Paris Siete. She had been given permission to build a small house, in which she was perfectly happy. I painted on the roof, away from her windows, off to the side where we could not see each other. Sometimes she came out and sat in the sun. She never bothered me, never asked questions, never stood behind me to look at what I was doing. Nor did we ever invade each other's territory. She made her living as an osteopath, manipulating the muscles of men and women in their own homes. Her ministrations appeared to be helpful, for she had a large clientele. She was probably in her middle fifties then. She was overweight, although most of the extra poundage was not fat but pure muscle. She left a note for me whenever she had time for tea. We always enjoyed our talks on everything and everyone from the ruins of Mitla to the murals of Diego Rivera.

One day, Madame Sonja, as she was known, asked if I would accompany her on a visit to a former patient who was living in a village called Ajijic, on Lake Chapala. She would pay all the expenses. The patient, Holga Menha, was desperately ill; Madame Sonja was the only one who could help him. He was a former dancer from Russia. We went by bus. I do not remember how long it took to reach Guadalajara, but it must have been nine or ten hours. We spent the night there and went on to Ajijic the next morning over a bumpy road.

There was not much to Ajijic, a village of 3,000 or so on Lake Chapala. There were no luxuries in Ajijic then, unless you would consider the Hotel Chapala, some five miles away, luxurious. The small pension in the center of Ajijic had rooms for us.

Late that first afternoon, Madame Sonja and I took a stroll along the beach to leave a note for Zara Alexeyeva Ayenara, adopted sister of the patient, announcing Madame Sonja's arrival in Ajijic and saying that she would attend her patient at nine the next morning. My knowledge of Spanish was limited, but I worked at studying it every day.

It was evening. The sun was setting but was still rearranging its various colors more and more garishly over the whole sky. Madame Sonja and I were walking along the edge of the lake. The water was reflecting the colors of the sky. Just then, when the sky was still brilliantly lit, a gate opened in front of us. A horse and rider came out. "It is Zara Alexeyeva Ayenara," whispered Madame Sonja. She was a ghostly figure in flowing silks and gossamer. She wore a wide-brimmed hat and held herself erect with a perfectly straight back. A long, thick rope-like braid of hair hung down to her waist. She led the horse into the lake and got off when the horse was in about two feet of water. She removed her outer garment and her hat and handed them to her *mozo*, who had been following slowly behind her. Her inner gown was her bathing garment. The *mozo* led the horse back to the beach. Neither Madame Sonja nor I said anything but her name. Soon, the swimmer returned and mounted the horse with the help of her *mozo* and returned home.

I never saw Holga. While waiting for Sonja to finish her therapy with him, I sat in one of the drawing rooms, which was decorated with frescoes of clouds and cherubs, like those that populate the paintings of Tiepolo and Correggio. Madame Sonja was not happy with Holga's appearance or with his response to her manipulations. He never came out of his room. There was no point to the therapy, she said to me, no point in continuing a treatment that was not helping. She decided to return to Mexico City, and I went with her. We had been in Ajijic for only ten days, but the walks I took alone or with Madame Sonja or with one of the residents of the village convinced me that Ajijic would be a good place for me to sit and paint for a year or so.

According to Madame Sonja, La Russa, as we all called Zara, was an American, born in Pennsylvania. She had become involved with Holga and agreed to be adopted as his sister in the Russian manner. In this way, there never were any difficulties in their sharing a room. It was then that her name was changed. They had been living together for a number of years, but gossip had it that they never slept in the same bed and there was never any sign of sexual activity.

There were only a handful of foreigners in Ajijic then. Ernesto Linares, or Lynn as we knew him, was a tall, blond, handsome young German who had been born in Guadalajara. He had inherited a considerable amount of farmland on the outskirts of Ajijic, but he spent most of his time painting in a drip technique that might have preceded the work of Jackson Pollock. He later committed suicide. In order to fit his six-foot, four-inch body into the coffin, it was necessary to cut off his feet at the ankles. A bulky woman named Esther, who drank rum by the glassful, also committed suicide in Ajijic, but not during my time there. She was well known, probably because of her habit of lifting her skirts and squatting down in the street whenever she needed to pee. A German brother and sister ran the small pension. They were nondescript and almost never talked to each other or to any of the guests. An elderly British couple, the Johnsons, had a splendid garden with hundreds of blossoming hibiscus. Also living close by was Neil James, who had published several books with titles like *Petticoat Vagabond in Lapland* and *Petticoat Vagabond among the Hairy Ainu*. Her most famous book was *Dust on My Heart*. Finally, there was Sam, one of the Barrymore clan. He was an alcoholic, a remittance man who appeared in Ajijic periodically.

After my return to Ajijic from Mexico City, other foreigners came to stay, notably Nikolas Muzenic, with whom I fell in love. He had been a student of Josef Albers at Black Mountain College. Albers himself arrived one afternoon, accompanied by his wife, Anni. They spent a couple of nights in Ajijic. Nikolas, alas, fell in love with Lynn, not with me. It was a disastrous affair that started out as if it would last forever. Nikolas remained in Ajijic for about two years. It wasn't long after he left Ajijic for California that he was found dead in his house, victim of a massive heart attack.

A year or more after my return to Ajijic from Mexico City, I was walking along the beach. It was dark, and I think Nikolas was with me. Zoe, a former lover of Henry Miller, had asked La Russa if she could practice on her piano. La Russa agreed. Nikolas and I had gone out, hoping to hear her play. We were sitting on the beach when the music began, Chopin études at first, then Bach, and ending up back with Chopin. She stumbled at first and replayed several passages, but it wasn't long before her fingers loosened and she played very well. During the Bach, the gate to La Russa's property opened, and we saw La Russa emerge, wearing her usual gowns that flowed with her movements. She walked to the edge of the lake, bent down as if in homage to the gods of the lake, and then began to move in dance. She ran down the beach with an exquisite sense of refinement and a complete understanding for the music, and then ran back to where we sat. She leaped and turned with astonishing grace. She was beautiful. She was magical. In the darkness, she seemed to float, as if Holga were with her, holding her, lifting her, carrying her with such ease and elegance that she might have been a great dancer, another Danilova.

That dance might have been the last performance of Zara Alexeyeva Ayenara. With the death of her brother, she lost her strength. She might have taught to help her through a financial crisis, but she turned her back on dance and returned to her books on theosophy, reading and rereading Madam Blavatska and Ouspensky. She disappeared into her house and came out only on rare occasions. I missed knowing that she would appear once again on the beach. She was an integral part of the life of Ajijic.

I lived in Ajijic for about three years and had one-man shows in Mexico City and in Guadalajara with the help of Carlos Merida. Every once in a while, Nikolas or Lynn would propose a trip to Manzanillo or to Tepic or to the Yucatán. Sometimes we went simply to get away from Ajijic; sometimes we collected artifacts, and sometimes we collected orchids. It was on those short trips that I found myself excited by the feel of the forest. It seemed to draw me unto itself so that I was almost compelled to go farther, deeper. The forest itself gave me a sense of freedom, a sense of being without restraints of any kind, inside a lush land that brought back memories of places to which I had never been.

It was near the end of my time in Mexico that I went with a friend to visit the Lacandón Indians, about whom I had recently read. The year must have been 1949 or 1950. They were a Maya people who were still living, the article said, traditional lives. We took various buses from Ajijic south to San Cristóbal de las Casas in the state of Chiapas. From there, we flew in a small overloaded plane to a village that may have been called Ocosingo and continued on by horseback. It is difficult now to reconstruct the thoughts I had then, so many years ago, going into a different world, one that was almost unknown. We left our horses and walked on silently, the only noise coming from the cracking of dried twigs beneath our feet. This

Introduction

was not the jungle, not the forest primeval of Bomba or Tarzan, but it was wild and beautiful.

Mexico was the catalyst for me. As I learned to settle the pounding in my chest, to settle my emotional life, I began to absorb and grow through the people and the land.

Suddenly, the Lacandón men were there around us, standing in trees, six or seven of them, dressed in dirty-white tunics, each with bow and arrows in hand. They did not seem threatening, although at first they looked ferocious. Their black hair was unkempt, as though it had never seen brush or comb. They appeared calm and curious, not violent in any way. Our guide was a Chamula who hailed his friends and said that we were visitors from a distant land. They spoke a language I did not understand. If possible, our guide told them, we would like to visit their village and perhaps sleep and eat there in exchange for goods. We had our own hammocks.

Just then, before moving from that astonishing scene of armed men standing in trees, before moving from that place to the house in which they lived, a memory flashed back to me as I looked up. I was in Coney Island once again, my mother and my two brothers around me. We were passing a line of tented side shows, one of which held a huge sign announcing the appearance of the Wild Man of Borneo. Underneath the lettering was a painting of a hairy creature in a cage. It squatted there, motionless. I think it was in a cage, but I am not certain. I may have been five or six at the time. It is the earliest memory of my childhood. I cannot now evoke the true image of this being, only that it appeared to be fierce. Now, again, it is in front of me, close up, staring at me just as I am staring back. The long hair is unbrushed and reaches below the shoulders. Bits of organic material are stuck in its hair. The cheeks are deeply hollowed out, cheekbones protruding. It is naked in my memory, but that could not have been. Perhaps it was not human but some other kind of primate. I do not recall the smell that must have emanated from whatever it was. I reached out to touch that vision, but it remained unclear, unformed. It was never real.

We did not stay long, only two or three days. My memory again fails when I try to identify the group of houses on the map. The village of Nahá seems too far from the ruins of Bonampak, our next destination.

The combination of my recollection of the Wild Man of Borneo and the Lacandón meant the beginning of a new life for me. The intensity of that experience marked the path I would follow for the next fifty years. I became obsessed with looking for a people who would accept me, teach me how to live without a feeling of aloneness, teach me love and allow for my sexuality. I did not articulate these needs to myself. It was enough that I searched in distant lands for romantic love and sex with men. I did not know then that there were many others who fit into the same category as myself, who suffered from not being "normal," whatever that is.

When I returned to New York from Mexico, I began working for my friends Richard and Floriano at their silk-screen greeting-card company, Tiber Press. I worked there for three or four months a year, folding Christmas cards and drawing some of the designs. It was ideal for me. I worked during the season and traveled or painted during the rest of the year. I had met them through another friend, Vance Bourjaily. He and I had done a children's book together; that is, he had written the captions while I had painted the watercolors. It was called *The Girl in the Abstract Bed,* a title that came from an abstract painting I had done for Vance and his wife, Tina. I had often baby-sat for their daughter, Anna. The painting was designed as the headboard of the crib. The book was, in truth, a portfolio of watercolors with a short delightful text by Vance. He took the mock-up of the book to Richard and Floriano, who immediately accepted it for publication.

Several artists went to Floriano to learn silk-screen techniques. Among the long list of those who studied with him were Andy Warhol, Stuart Davis, and Charles Sheeler. In fact, it was Floriano who taught Warhol how to duplicate a dollar bill.

Richard and Floriano had met in Rome while Richard was working there for the United States government on the Marshall Plan. When they decided to live together for the rest of their lives, Floriano came to the United States and took a job that gave him the beginnings of silk-screen techniques. They set up a company called Tiber Press, which printed Christmas cards. Floriano modified and developed printing techniques in a way that quickly attracted a group of artists who came to be known as the Second Generation of the New York School of Abstract Expressionism.

Tiber Press also produced a huge 17½- by 14-inch four-volume edition of original silk screens paired with work of various poets. Each volume contained the work of one poet and one painter: Frank O'Hara was paired with Michael Goldberg; Jimmy Schyler, with Grace Hartigan; and Kenneth Koch, with Alfred Leslie.

At the same time, Tiber was publishing *Folder,* a literary magazine in portfolio format with short fiction, poetry, photographs, and paintings by unknowns who became very well known a few years later. Stanley Marcus sent an original Ben Shawn of Martin Luther, asking if Floriano could copy it in silk screen and make it into a Christmas card. It came out marvelously well.

I was a painter in those days. I had my first one-man show in New York in 1953 at the Ganso Gallery. When it closed, the Peridot took me on, and

Introduction

I had seven or eight exhibitions there until the owner died. The gallery was then bought by a dealer who sold only work from the 1920s and 1930s. I used my journeys as source material for my painting. I went to Greece for a year and made drawings and watercolors that I later translated into oils on canvas. On another trip, I went to Italy to look at art. In Florence, I ran to the Uffizi to visit the drawing collection. For years before my first trip to Europe, I had been steeping myself in Renaissance drawings and looked forward to seeing so many of them at the Uffizi. I was shocked and disappointed to see a sign at the entrance to the drawing collection, saying *Chiuso*. I was so upset I could not contain myself and knocked on the door. A uniformed man came out and asked if he could help me. I told him that I was a student of drawings of the Renaissance. I had come all the way from America just to see the Uffizi collection, only to find it closed. He looked very sympathetic when he realized that tears were streaming down my cheeks. I spoke only a few words of Italian then, but my story easily got through to him. He said, "Just a moment, signor." He closed the door and soon returned to invite me in. I was introduced to the woman who was the curator of the collection. I told my story once again, which again included tears that I could not stop. The curator said, "Please write down the names of ten painters whose works you would like to see." My brain went blank, but soon I had my list: Piero della Francesca, Uccello, Michelangelo, Giotto, Giovanni Bellini, Gentile Bellini, Bronzino, Andrea Mantegna, Pollaiuolo, and Correggio. These were the first ten names to enter my head. The curator looked at the list and said, "Please come back tomorrow morning at 9:15." In my excitement. I was there almost an hour early, but I did not knock on the door until two or three minutes before 9:15. The guard ushered me in and took me to a small room with two tables. A few minutes later, he wheeled in two carts filled with portfolios. The attendant excused himself and left me alone with hundreds of drawings.

I took the first portfolio to the table and opened it. Michelangelo! A chill ran through my whole back. I could hear, as well as feel, my heart pounding. I picked up the first drawing. There was no glass, no plastic, no frame, no mounting. There was nothing between my eyes and the drawing itself. I turned the drawing over and examined it. There was the beginning of a drawing there. My hands began to shake. Is it real? Is this truly what I know it is? Is it possible that I am really holding a Michelangleo in my hands? I spent that day looking at one masterwork after another. I did not get through half the Michelangelo drawings, let alone the others still awaiting my inspection. That evening, I asked if I could come back the next day. The curator said, "You may come back any time. The drawings will remain here until you are finished." I spent the whole of my first week in Florence looking at works that astonished me, particularly the Uccellos, the Giottos, and the Mantegnas.

I traveled farther.

I sat atop a truck that took me from Tripoli in Libya to Faya Largeau in Chad. I crossed the Sahara from north to south. Another truck went as far as the Central African Republic and still another to Brazzville in the Congo. I traveled slowly through Ethiopia and Somalia. The longest trip was the one I spent crossing Asia, taking two years to go from Istanbul to Singapore and then to Borneo and the Philippines.

In 1954, I saw an exhibition at the Museum of Modern Art that included three photographs of Machu Picchu that instantly compelled me to go. The photographs were breathtaking. The ruins themselves were in the most stunning landscape imaginable. When I decided to apply for a Fulbright Fellowship, I chose Peru as my goal.

I was always looking for a barbaric place, one in which I could settle down and draw and metaphorically take in the environment, as well as the people. Every new place was more elemental than the previous one. I went to Peru without the anxiety within me that was usually part of the way in which I searched out myself. And when I was told of people who lived in the forest on the eastern side of the Andes, I not only longed to go but had a powerful need to live among them. I knew nothing of who they were, those who lived there. "Keep the river on your right," I was told. It was the beginning of my place, the beginning of the journey that contradicted my early life.

In my grant application, I had written of my interest in the archaeology of Peru, of the great ruins of the Inca and other peoples of the Andes, but when I heard that there were people still living in the jungle, I changed direction and boarded a truck that took me down the mountainside. It was there that I had my first real encounter with the essential, basic part of my existence.

It was a strange and frightening time, yet it was neither strange nor frightening. It was not alien or even different in any way. It was neither odd nor freakish. It was simply a time of meeting my own vision of the Harakhambut in my own vision of them. The excitement of being face to face with the image I had chosen in my childhood for my own identity was overpowering. The look of surprise and pleasure on the faces of the men seemed to reflect what I hoped was on my own face, my own body. The wonder of their trying to remove my clothes to see who I was stimulated and exhilarated me, tantalized me. It was a remarkable moment, one I cherish, even today. Their faces were painted red, and their bodies painted with black linear designs that I could not understand. The women were hidden at that time, but they came out later. The designs on their bodies were completely different from those on the men, with large areas painted black. It gave the women the look of wearing long black gloves with décolleté dresses.

There seemed to be a passivity among the men. They touched my bare skin with the tips of their fingers. We laughed a lot and then walked an hour to their house. I stayed with them for months, until the day when violence became overt and dangerous. They offered me human flesh, and I ate a small piece. I soon left them and never thought to return. I did go back, however, although I am still unable to approach that aspect of myself that I had always kept hidden, the violence that I suppose is in all of us. The years were 1955 and 1956.

The Asmat, too, were cannibals.

I was determined to go to New Guinea from the first moment I heard of the disappearance of Michael Rockefeller. He had gone down to Asmat from the Jayawijaya Mountains of Irian Jaya, the western half of the island of New Guinea. Michael was the sound engineer for a film called *Dead Birds,* being made among the Dani people. The year was 1961. The catamaran in which he preferred to travel through the swamps of Asmat turned over at the mouth of the Betsj River. Two local people who were with him jumped in to swim ashore for help. The fourth person in the party was René Wassing, the Dutch district officer, who could not swim. Michael, however, is said to have been an exceptional swimmer. The following morning, when it appeared to him that help was not coming, Michael decided to go for help himself. He jumped in the river, and that was the last anyone heard of him, except for vague rumors of his being killed and eaten. The carvings he had collected were originally meant for the Museum of Primitive Art, but most of them were too large to be stored there, let alone be part of an exhibition. The museum was then on Fifty-fourth Street in two side-by-side townhouses. In 1962, the carvings were put on display at the Museum of Modern Art, which is where I first saw them and had my first taste of Asmat artifacts. That exhibition alone would have been enough to incite me into going to Asmat. The power and ferocity of the carvings, in fact, invaded my dreams and kept me from sleeping for the next several days. After the show at the Museum of Modern Art, the carvings were sent to the Rockefeller family estate in Pocantico Hills, New York, where they were put in storage until many of them went on permanent display in the Michael Rockefeller Wing of the Metropolitan Museum of Art.

It took me almost ten years to get to Asmat. I went first in 1973 after a long period of saving the money and then waiting for an available seat on the small Cessna that flew down from Sentani on the northern coast of

Irian. I met Bishop Alphonse Sowada, who was from St. Cloud, Minnesota. He was a particularly interesting man. Together with Father Frank Trenkenschuh, they had raised money to build a museum designed for the local people, not for the nonexistent tourist. After a few weeks of travel, I decided to find a way to stay in Asmat for some months or years. I asked the bishop if anyone was working on the card catalog of the 2,000 pieces in the collection. He answered that no one in Asmat knew how to put together a catalog. I asked if it would be possible for me to return to New York, work with registrars at the American Museum of Natural History and the Metropolitan Museum of Art to learn their systems of cataloging, and then come back to Asmat as a volunteer. I am sure the bishop must have said to himself, "This guy will never do what he says, and I will almost certainly never hear from him again, so I might just as well say yes."

Unlike Neil Armstrong, who stepped out of the past when he opened the door of his lunar module and moved into the future when he stepped down onto the surface of the moon, I stepped from the present back into the past when I stepped from the Cessna into a canoe. Instead of living disparate lives, I went on only the one path: there was the world of art in the carvings of the Asmat and farther on into the world of art with my drawings of more than 300 of the museum's artifacts; there was the world of writing the books that I was publishing; there was the world of anthropology that I was recording in my journal and in publications; and, finally, there was the world of sexual excitement.

The men were magnificent creatures, their upper bodies hard and sinewy, but their legs comparatively thin. The men gained their marvelous musculature through paddling their canoes every day, their bodies so beautiful that I could not at times resist touching them intimately. Their bodies were always bared for all to see. There was never any violent reaction to my touch, never any sense of shock. There was only acceptance and pleasure at my approach. The sensuality of the men was phenomenal. So it was that all my worlds came together in Asmat. Suddenly, those four separate parts of my life were blending into a cohesive unit, one life, one being.

1

The Origins of As-Atat

I have lived at least two lives: one in New York, the other in Asmat. New York is where I was born and where I grew up, the place from which I made forays into distant parts of the world. New Guinea is something else, a place to which I have now been going for more than twenty-five years. It is not the New Guinea of Bronisław Malinowski or Margaret Mead or Gregory Bateson; instead, it is the New Guinea of lesser known but no less brilliant lights, such as A. A. Gerbrands, Father Gerard Zegwaard, and Bishop Alphonse Sowada. My two lives are completely separate from each other, each lived intensely and fully, although I now spend much more time in New York than in New Guinea. In Asmat, I live for the most part without what we think of as the amenities of life: no television, no radio, no fruit, no beef, hardly ever any vegetables. I live in a swamp, among the Asmat people. I sleep on a mat of pandanus leaves on a flooring of tree bark. I eat sago, sometimes with peanut butter and jelly that I have brought along. In certain remote areas, when the men are naked, I, too, am naked, except for sneakers. It is surely too late for the soles of my feet to adjust to the rough floor of the forest.

My journal is in my lap, dated April 12, 1976, As-Atat. The men's house in which I am staying with Father Johnny Fleischhacker is dense with smoke and smells strongly of tobacco laced with cloves and other spices. Everyone is smoking, including the youngest children there, aged four or five. The fires, built on beds of caked mud, are used for roasting sago, shrimp, and other foods put directly onto the embers. No pots or pans or other cooking utensils are visible; the people of As-Atat have not yet learned their use and do not have the wherewithal to buy them, for they have not yet come into a cash economy. The fires take away the night chill and will soon be banked well enough to emit no smoke. The glowing embers give enough light for the men to move around without disturbing the spirits that normally leave the sleeping bodies of men, women, and children. The life spirit leaves the body when it sleeps. It wanders at will, wherever it chooses, and returns to the body before daybreak. To step over someone who is sleeping often leads to the death of that person, for that one stride over the body prevents the spirit from returning to its home in the living being.

With two Caucasian men there, me and Father Fleischhacker, with so much tobacco around, and with so many trade items passing from hand to hand, no one feels like sleeping. Just as the men are interested in looking at us, talking and listening, and feeling the texture of the clothing we wear, so are we engrossed in the exchange of material goods for carvings. Each artifact—each drum, war shield, paddle, spear, figure carving—is dedicated to someone who has recently died. Some of the men wear ragged shorts, but most are naked except for the spiraled shell nosepiece worn through the septum and the dangling dog-tooth necklaces, both signs of a man who has taken a head in battle. Dogs are part of the family household and are used for hunting wild boar or cassowary, and even humans in the past.

We are still trading at ten o'clock at night, although in the dim light I prefer putting off most transactions until morning, when judging the artifacts will be easier. Drums can then be noted as having been used for years simply by the look and feel of the wood's texture and the absence of sharp edges to the figures carved into the handle. Other artifacts are not so easily recognized in the dark as being old and used. I am always searching out old artifacts whose carvers have had as little influence from the outside world as possible. Even then, during my earliest months in Asmat, I could quickly see that the spirit of the carvings had changed and not for the better. They no longer have the illusive spiritual quality that is present in most carvings of the past. There is no use trying to explain this conceptualization to anyone, let alone explain it to myself. It is as though the carver and the spirit of the dead man for whom the carving would be named spoke to each other in whispers, softly, in order to tender to each other's needs. Surely, that spirit was close by, perhaps to induce some particularly personal element through which the man's family could recognize him. Contact with one's deceased relatives is only natural. The living want to avenge the dead; the dead want to go on in peace to the Land of the Dead.

The Origins of As-Atat

Darkness had already come three and a half hours earlier, bringing with it any number of spirits, good and evil. Everyone seems wide awake, anxious to acquire a machete or a steel ax or to be given more tobacco. Only one man is lying on his sleeping mat. The men sit with straight backs, their legs folded up, elbows on knees, in the attitude of a praying mantis about to copulate. It is one of the Asmat head-hunting symbols, carved in relief on war shields and on other types of artifacts, for the female mantis devours the male during intercourse.

I am on "patrol" with Father Fleischhacker, who has invited me to the outer reaches of his parish to collect artifacts for the museum in Agats, capital of the area. Johnny is a jolly, relatively short man from Minnesota. He is somewhat overweight and has a delightful sense of humor. We get along very well. I am writing here continually. Everything around me is new and exciting and must go into my journal as quickly as possible or I forget it. At first, Johnny does all the talking and asks all the questions while I write down the names of carvers, the various uses of the war shields, the meanings of the symbols incised on them, and the names of the objects in both Indonesian and Asmat. I record the names of the rivers on which we travel upstream from Jamasj, Father Fleischhacker's home village. I even note what we ate for supper (canned Spam and boiled rice), what the reception had been like at arrival (wonderfully noisy and welcoming), how many had attended Mass that evening (fifty-six in this village of a couple of hundred), and how Johnny had conducted his brief clinic, mostly giving injections of penicillin for yaws, with its terrible open sores and lesions. He also dispensed chloroquine to those with malaria, an endemic illness. Although the Asmat have almost no experience with doctors or with Western medication, they have no fear of swallowing pills or getting injections. Both the men and the women have great respect for him both as a priest and as someone who normally could cure illnesses. Penicillin works quickly with yaws, within a few days, in fact.

I have been in Asmat for a year, working as a volunteer at the museum in Agats. I immerse myself as deeply as possible in Asmat culture without actually committing myself to learning the physical aspects of life. There is no way I can learn to chop down a sago tree or do any of the common tasks of men's daily life. But I collect artifacts and information on symbolism and on the use of the carvings. I catalog the objects and work with Eric Sarkol, the curator's assistant, designing and mounting displays. Eric has a romantic look about him, with his long, curly, densely black hair and full mustache. He wears horn-rimmed glasses and has considerable drawing ability. He is always modest about his looks. His family comes from the Kei Islands, off the western coast of Irian Jaya. Yuven Biakai, the curator, is an Asmat from the village of Ayam. He received some training at the East-

17

West Center in Honolulu, but is now reluctant to take down the exhibition that Eric and I put together. He may have done so by now.

I spend half my time traveling through Asmat and half at the museum in Agats, working on the card catalog, drawing many of the carvings, recording their statistics, and photographing them. I am determined to keep a proper record of my stay.

If I narrow down the world map to where the island of New Guinea can be found with relative ease, just north of Australia, I need another map to focus in on Asmat, in the southwestern part of the island, and still another map to locate Agats, Jamasj, As-Atat, and all the other villages I have visited. From Agats, Johnny and I, with three boatmen, cross the immense Flamingo Bay in a thirty-five-foot mappi boat, named for the Dutch craft that first sailed the Mappi River, east of Asmat. Jamasj is on the western side of the Pomatsj River, one of the three great waterways that empty into Flamingo Bay. We spend two nights in Jamasj and go farther upstream the next morning. We turn from one river into another, ending up on the Kar at As-Atat. On small rivers and streams, we pass bivouacs, built in conical form like tipis, made from leaves of the nipa palms that line many narrow rivers. A smaller variety of pandanus, also used for roofing and bivouacs, line other streams.

As we travel on, the vegetation changes with each bend of the river. Short stretches of sandy beach as well as ornamental grasses appear. A profusion of orchids, other epiphytes, and parasites grow in the crotches of branches and tree trunks, but few are in bloom that I can see. Mangrove trees are covered with small white or yellow flowers, while the low-lying landscape is a mass of greens of various heights, a typical mangrove swamp.

The forest is never completely silent. The mappi's engine clucks and croaks and pounds away during the day, and at night, when the boat is anchored in the river, there are always animal or bird sounds. During the day, red-eyed black palm cockatoos shriek as they fly over in pairs, great flocks of white cockatoos burst out, and screeching hornbills flap their wings with great whooshing sounds, demonstrating why the Portuguese, the first Europeans to land on the island, took home the news that rhinoceros thrived here. They had misinterpreted the sound of flapping wings, confusing it with the sound of rhino hooves stamping through the undergrowth. Flocks of smaller birds fly up at the approach of the noisy boat. Only rarely do we see the tail of a crocodile as it slips into the muddy waters or see the "V" left by a snake swimming directly in front of us. Isolated egrets fly up ahead of us, land in trees, and fly up again as we approach.

Far upstream, fifty or fifty-five miles from Agats on the southern coast, massive banyan trees grow while ironwoods reach immense heights. Eagle wood grows there, too, one of the most expensive woods on earth, selling, they say, for as much as $4,000 a pound in Jeddah. It is later sold all over Saudi Arabia to those with harems, who use the chips of the wood as incense, said by some to be an effective aphrodisiac. I bought a few pieces for myself and burned them, but had no reaction that I could note.

The bird life, the animal life, the river, the forest and all the plant life, all the human life, the way the Asmat live and work, the way they commune with spirits of the dead through their carvings, the whole manner of their physical lives—all combine to form a way that I wanted to have lived myself. If we cannot change the past, we can imagine a past different from the one we lived. Throughout my life, I have been searching for a way to connect to other human beings and find that among people like the Asmat, who live in a world of spirits, I can lose my insecurities and be content. I watch the men of Asmat and try in some way to emulate them. At night, at times, we huddle and embrace.

When the bottom of the canoe is dry, I lie back, my head propped on a piece of baggage. I feel then like the descriptions I've heard from addicts when a needle goes into a vein and a syringeful of heroin is received. Or I sit up, lean against my patrol box, and watch the back of the thigh muscles of the naked paddler directly in front of me, pulsing, relaxing, tightening. I watch his buttocks roll, first one and then the other. I watch his back ripple, covered with dripping beads of sweat. I watch him lean forward and dip his paddle into the river to thrust the canoe forward, all six of the men dipping paddles simultaneously. As a sign of his own pleasure and satisfaction in the knowledge that he will soon have wages and a full plug of tobacco from me, he jumps up onto the gunwale of the canoe, easily balancing himself there. He clasps the upper edge of the canoe between the big and second toes of each foot. He takes up a long reed container, flicks it high above his head, tosses magical white powder made of burned and crushed mussel shells that hides us from enemies, and assures us that we are traveling quickly and will soon arrive at our destination.

I am always looking at the scene around me in the forest, and I am always watching the men in the men's house. In As-Atat, too, I watch the way the men sit or squat or stand on one leg, the other resting against the side of the knee, like a heron. I watch a man with a two- or three-year-old child clinging to his neck from behind, the child held there by the father's hands at his buttocks. I watch the way the men stretch out on the floor of the family house with their heads leaning into the laps of their wives, who are deftly knotting their husbands' hair into dreadlocks. I watch the men stand with their hands cupping their testicles without self-consciousness.

The women appeared at first not to have even the slightest interest in me, but later I learned that they had been dissembling, partly because of an innate shyness in front of strangers, partly because of the evil that they thought I might inflict on them or on one of their children, and partly because they were afraid that their husbands might notice their interest and beat them. To both men and women, Johnny Fleischhacker was an anomaly: He never seemed to have sexual intercourse and never made suggestions to the women. How was this possible? They reasoned that he must be having intercourse with one of the spirits, but they could not determine which one attracted him into such a high state of excitement. Even when I later stayed with a family that had invited me to spend the night, the women were given space away from me, sleeping and eating there. I was given only a slightly larger place for myself. It was the eldest wife who fed me, although she never handed food to me directly but always passed it to her husband, who passed it on to me. The women invariably hid their faces behind their hands and would not answer any questions. It was surely a failing of my own. Unlike the men, the women covered the pubic area with a small câche sex made of fibers from leaves of the sago palm.

The women gather most of the food; that is, they fish every morning for breakfast or go with their husbands and other relatives into the jungle to pound sago when it is low. The men are less active in the early morning, often preferring to sleep until their wives return from fishing and have sago and shrimp on the fire. The women also search out edible roots and plants. The men were the warriors and, in the past, did the hunting of animals and humans. It was their job to watch over their families when they were in the forest gathering food. The women and children were then at their most defenseless and subject to attack by their enemies. They were sometimes kidnapped and taken to enemy villages, where they might serve as slaves or even as wives of individual warriors. Or they might be killed and eaten. It was not unusual for an entire family to disappear in this way. Now, with the cessation of warfare, there is no longer a need for the protection that was so necessary to a man's esteem, although a tradition of the men protecting the women continues. They always take their weapons with them when they go into the forest.

Both men and women are involved in the making of sago in the forest. The family goes out in a dugout canoe to a bivouac on its own property and stays for a few days and nights. The men choose a likely looking sago palm (*Metroxylon*), test it by making a hole in the tree trunk, and bring out some of the pith to taste. If the sago is judged to be ready, the tree is cut down. Sago is the main food of the Asmat.

The men do the heavy work of chopping down the tree, and then opening it so that the women can begin to pound the pith. The men build the trough necessary for the processing of the food. The women pound, wash, and rinse the pith, and wait for the sago to settle and harden. They package the sago in leaves. A family of eight can make enough sago in one day to last from two to three weeks in the village. When the sago is ready, the family returns home or may stay on another week to fish and gather edible roots.

The rhythm of daily life gives the Asmat time to relax. Living in the bivouac is a time of freedom, when there are no government officials or merchants with prying eyes to disturb them. In the village, there is a certain amount of decorum, but in the bivouac they feel free and can do all the things they used to do without fear of punishment. The ritual of *papisj* is one of them. I have not talked with anyone in recent years who admits to having taken part in this rite. The practice has been prohibited by Christian missionaries and may no longer exist. *Papisj* is a rite whereby two male friends, who were bonded together in their youth through family ties, exchange wives in times of crisis. The crisis can be anything from an outbreak of cholera, causing the deaths of half the villagers, to continual warfare to someone's terrifying dream of death and destruction. Before the observances can begin, however, a man must ask his wife whether she approves of the exchange on a temporary basis. The woman not only must agree, but must have borne her husband at least one child. The wives may be exchanged for one night or for a longer time. An agreement on the timing is made before each woman goes to the house of her husband's partner.

Crises always occur when the cosmos is out of balance. There are two ways of stabilizing it. One is through warfare, avenging all deaths that have recently occurred; the other is through the flow of semen. Having sex with a relatively new partner renews the vigor of all participants.

There is still another relationship of sexual interest, one called *mbai*. This exists between two men who live along the southern coast of Asmat. The young initiates are probably put together in the same way as those in the *papisj* arrangement, except that it allowed for sexual activity between the men as well as between the men and the women.

Most men and women of the island believe in the great, magical power of semen. By ingesting it in one way or another—through fellatio or sodomy or rubbing it into the body of an initiate—an initiate will ensure himself of growing to manhood with all the qualities of a great warrior. The more semen he takes in, the faster and stronger will he grow. Some believe that this can be achieved only through fellatio; others believe that it happens only when sodomy is performed and semen is absorbed through the anus. Semen is but one of the body fluids with magical qualities. The other is menstrual blood, which may be used in rituals whose intent is to harm others.

Often, at night in a men's house far from government officials, police, missionaries, and traders, I think about this exchange of semen. I think about how it must influence the concept of masculinity held by many men and women in New Guinea. Tears well up, not tears of pain or sadness but tears of being at peace with myself, of contentment. I think about it, too, in New York, and I no longer look for answers to questions that have no answers. Life has such an astonishing variety of ways in which to play itself out in front of us. How lucky I am!

Am I part of some ancient race of ancient men, now weak and humble, feeding on youths to heal our bodies? Is it the Bible or is it simply custom that offers the blessing "May you live to be 120"? The reciprocity that seems natural in parts of New Guinea might now be reversed, so that ancients like myself might take in the semen of youths to give us strength enough to go on living. It suited me, just as it suited the Asmat to absorb unto themselves the sweat of my body, to run their hands over the streams of perspiration and wipe those hands on their own bodies, their own chests and faces, to take in the power and ferocity that they think I must have had in my youthful years.

I had never thought of body sweat as being anything but what it is: perspiration, slightly salty. But when I dance with the men in the men's house, I am on the edge of a trance from the beat of the drums, from shaking myself, shaking my hands and elbows in imitation of a cassowary, with the sweat pouring out of my body like the sweat on the bodies of the other men. I somehow feel elevated, as though I am on a drug that allows me to dance the whole night through. Imagine that sweat flying off the bodies of fifty men or more, and me standing still with my hands absorbing the juices flowing out of Donatus's body, out of Yuven's body. It feels like magic! It *is* magic. It is even spiritual.

During my first half-hour in As-Atat, I buy a bamboo horn carved in high relief with shell-nosepiece designs and two beautifully carved drums. There may be twenty adult men here, sitting in front of us, all crowded together, listening and commenting. Younger men and boys are in the back. All are exhilarated by our presence, the first visitors since Johnny was here on patrol six months earlier. They delight in watching the transfer of metal knives and fishhooks, nylon fishing line, and steel axes. I put out a plug of tobacco, which is immediately taken up by the headman, who pulls off small pieces that he passes around. Each man loosens the tobacco and rolls it in a paper of nipa leaf. Soon, the tobacco is gone, and I replace it with another plug. The Asmat feel relaxed and content when they are smoking, more so after having been without tobacco since Johnny's last visit.

The Asmat love to tell stories and listen to others telling tales of bygone days, stories they all have heard many times before. For the most part, they talk of the dead and how they came to die. They talk about spirits of the living and spirits of the dead.

Before starting on this trip with Johnny, I had been on a journey far upstream, to the Brazza River and to other areas close by. The year was 1975. Few travelers had been there then, some missionaries and merchants looking for crocodile skins—but literally only a handful had gone there. They had caught only glimpses of the local people, who easily hid from them. The people of the Brazza River are closely related to the Asmat, who live farther downstream, and, indeed, have been called Asmat for a number of years, although they remain on the outer fringes of Asmat territory. I could not speak their language, but many of the words having to do with artifacts were the same: *em* for "drum"; *jamasj* or *jemesj* for "shield." The shields, in fact, had many symbols carved into their surfaces, including the flying fox, a common motif found throughout Asmat.

Unlike the naked Asmat, who never wore anything to cover the penis, the men of the Brazza pushed the body of the penis back into the scrotum and tied a small fresh leaf over the foreskin, their own sense of modesty. The men of As-Atat were amused but could not understand the need for the leaf, particularly since it had to be removed in order to urinate. Perhaps their low intake of fresh water precluded their need to micturate. In the days when all the men of coastal Asmat were naked, they wore only decorations of necklaces, cuscus-fur headbands with feathers of the sulphur-crested cockatoo, nosepieces, arm- and leg bands of rattan, and dance belts with feathers of the cassowary that covered the buttocks, leaving the penis completely bare and unencumbered. Even as late as 1976, many of the men were still naked, except for body ornamentation.

Penis coverings in central Asmat as a whole were varied and included an astonishing assortment of phallic trappings. On my first journey to the Brazza, I took a side trip up the relatively narrow Dairam Hitam River, where the men of every village indicated their modesty in different ways. One group wore a ring of woven rattan around the corona like a wedding band on a finger; another tightly fit a tube of rattan over the whole body of the penis, leaving the head exposed. Still another covered only the tip of the penis with a small nut, while in a village no more than half a mile upstream, the body of the penis was enclosed in rattan tubing, with the head concealed by a leaf. Farther upstream, the men wore only a shell over the very tip of the penis. All were held up or straight out by a string that went from the corona to the waist. It was easy enough, after a while, to identify the village from which a man came simply by looking at his groin. I did a few drawings to show the men what the penises looked like. Alas, I had no camera on that trip.

All this within a distance of no more than the two miles between Tiau and Djemu. Elsewhere, on the fringes of Asmat, men wore hornbill beaks or gourd penis sheaths of varying lengths; still farther afield, in the mountains, the men wore curlicued gourds, straight gourds, fat gourds, and thin gourds, in addition to the shells and strings used to hold the penis in what appears to be semierection. The few women to be seen were dressed and ornamented with loops of cassowary quill or bamboo plugs for ear decoration and nosepieces made of the second wing bones of flying foxes threaded with the breasts of capricorn beetles, all very much the same as one another. Short skirts or girdles of twisted sago leaf were tied around the waist to cover the area of the groin and the buttocks.

Paulus Asmisi, the *dewan paroki,* or head of the parish council, of As-Atat, says he does not remember ever having had to make fire. Fire is rarely allowed to go out. If a disaster occurs, it is always possible to borrow fire from a relative or a neighbor. No one seemed to remember how it was made in the past. Both men and women carry it with them wherever they go, even taking it in the dugout when they travel into the forest, keeping it in the bottom of the canoe on a base of mud on long journeys. They heat sago in the fire and light their cigarettes. Matches sometimes find their way upstream, but they quickly disappear during celebrations when a man might show off his wealth by using them.

The Asmat are always asking about other peoples of the area, but no questions were asked about my life or Johnny's life or even about where we came from. Were they simply being polite? Or did they consider such questions to be immodest?

When Paulus was as young as the men presently behind him in the men's house, he always sat there and listened to the stories of the older men. He heard them over and over again and can repeat them verbatim whenever the occasion arises.

"Yes, I will tell you a story about how we Asmat came to be here," said Paulus. He shifted his buttocks into a more comfortable position and began: "After the big flood, after all the land was covered with water for many days, all fire was extinguished. People were hungry because they couldn't cook their sago or fish. This happened on the River of Shit, the Kali As. Everyone went looking for fire, all the men, all the women, all the children. Finally, flames were found on top of a tree belonging to Biwiripitsj. Biwiripitsj is the name of one of our first ancestors. He tried to climb the tree, but the branches were twisted in so many directions that he could not get through to the top and had to give up. Many people tried and failed."

Paulus sat with his legs crossed, almost whispering the story. It was difficult for me to hear, although everyone, even those in the rear, heard and understood every word. Their ears were as sharp as their eyes. When

Paulus paused to light or relight a cigarette, I would ask what had been said and then would put it into my journal.

"A small python," Paulus went on, "came along. The men asked it to climb the tree and bring down the fire. Everyone was hungry and needed fire to cook their food. The snake was so much thinner than all the men that it was able to climb and wiggle his way through the branches. He caught the fire in his mouth and brought it down. The python gave it to everyone, spreading it among all the people of Asmat. They were the first real people.

"Now, there were three men from As-Atat. They were among those given fire. It was not really the python that gave them the fire, but Biwiri-pitsj, who owned the tree where the fire was found. It was his tree, and it was his fire. They went to a bivouac that belonged to a man from Jamasj. Jamasj and As-Atat were enemies at that time. The three men were happy with the fire. They started burning the walls with torches to chase out the bad spirits. They had the fire and wanted to put it to good use right away. They burned the walls of the feast house, rubbing the walls up and down with the torches. One of the men from Jamasj started hitting the people of As-Atat with firewood. He was jabbing them with his spear. He pushed the spear into a man's body and killed him.

"All the small villages were frightened of Jamasj and decided to band together. Then they were all part of one village and were all enemies of Ja-masj. Men came and took the body of the man who had just been killed back to Jamasj. The Jamasj people saw the body with the spear sticking out and were ready to take revenge. The fight took place in Jamasj village itself.

"During the fight, three canoes from Jamasj took off to the jungle where they met Djitatim of As-Atat. Djitatim was hunting wild boar with his spear and his dogs. Djitatim's son was also out hunting. He was hunting white cockatoo nearby for their feathers. Djitatim knew there was trouble because his brother-in-law had been killed. He knew that he would be killed by the people of Jamasj taking revenge. The Jamasj people denied that they wanted to kill him, but they would take revenge, even though they said they would not kill him. Djitatim knew that the people of Jamasj always lied and would certainly kill him if he did not do something to prevent it. To appease them, even though they said they would not kill him, Djitatim gave them all his food and asked them to kill him later. Djitatim knew that it was taboo for the people of Jamasj to kill him after he had said this and after he gave them food."

Paulus never lost the thread of his story. We would have known immediately had he done so, for there would have been the shouts of correction by the older men. The slightest deviation from the original story might cause anger.

Listening was like being back in the synagogue when the day's portion of the Torah was being read aloud and every mispronunciation was angrily corrected. Paulus had no need to write anything down, no need to know how to write or read. His memory was faultless. His whole manner, his enunciation, the look on his face, the absolute lack of hesitation, reflected his vast knowledge of As-Atat and its history.

"The Jamasj people," Paulus continued, "asked Djitatim where his son was. He was in the forest hunting white cockatoo. They would kill him instead of Djitatim, they said. Djitatim went to the forest to find him. He called to his son, and together they went to Jamasj. When the people of As-Atat heard that Djitatim and his son had gone to Jamasj, they set about crying and wailing. They knew that one of the men would be killed. Djitatim asked the Jamasj people, 'Are you going to kill us now?' 'No,' they said. 'We are not going to kill you, but we are going to kill your son .' Then they killed him. They cut off his testicles and his penis, his fingers and his toes. They stuck the parts in the ground, thereby opening the way to a new river.

"Djitatim asked for the body so it would not be eaten, and they gave it to him. He took it in his *perahu* to As-Atat. There was peace, and no one was planning revenge."

The Asmat usually ate the bodies of enemies they had killed. They often severed the head before arriving back at their own village. It was put into the fire to burn away the flesh and hair, as well as to cook the brains, which were given to the elderly to eat, to strengthen them. The chiefs, too, were often given a portion of the brains. The rest of the body was cut up according to certain rites handed down through the mythological ancestors of the Asmat: Biwiripitsj and Desoipitsj. The arms and legs were cut off, and then the torso was taken apart in the specific manner taught to them by their ancestral heroes, the same way they had been taught to slaughter pigs and other animals.

Intimate understanding of the region was necessary to everyone in Asmat. They had named every river, every tributary, every stream, every runnel, every rill. Not only did they know every aspect of every waterway, but they knew who owned what section and who owned the trees of the forest. Invasion of these territories and the stealing of fish or sago or fruit or any of the animals within the forest led directly to war.

Paulus went on: "That night, the war chief of As-Atat told the people to gather sago the following day. By then, the body of Djitatim's son was beginning to stink in the canoe.

"The three men of As-Atat put the body on a platform. The women of

26

the house of the deceased began to wail. They stripped themselves bare and rolled in the mud to hide the smells of their bodies from the spirit of the deceased. If the spirit recognized the smell, it would enter the body of the relative and begin to control it."

When the Asmat returned from a successful head-hunting raid, they blew their horns as they approached their village. The sound announced to everyone that all heads and bodies were in the canoes. Many on shore were able to distinguish the pitch of the horn and could therefore recognize the man blowing it. The women, the children, and the old people lined the bank of the river, shouting and throwing missiles of spears, branches, rotten fruit, and balls of mud at the returning men in mock battle.

"They took the bodies to As-Atat and ate them," Paulus continued. "They decided to move because they had depleted the supply of sago where they were and because the scouts had seen a good place to settle.

"After a while the people of As-Atat came back to their original site and established a permanent village where we are now. The government has said that if we want a school and a teacher, we must stay in one place and not move with the sago. We came from the forest. We came from deep in the forest. It was our ancestors who brought us here. They lived upriver from Biwar Laut. No one knew that the headman was a woman. It was she who bore our ancestors. Everyone thought she was a man because she wore a star stone ax affixed to her girdle. It was a four-pointed star, with one of the points protruding from the bottom of the girdle like a penis. Everyone thought it was a penis."

Paulus told still another story late that same night. He was inexhaustible.

"There was an old man named Koko," said Paulus. "When a coconut tree was as high as my knees, Koko climbed the tree with a rolled stick of sago in his hands. He told the tree to grow up to the skies. Koko said, 'Good. I'll climb you and pick the stars.' Koko did so and climbed and picked the stars with his stick of sago. Koko was going around picking the stars and the sago. All through the night, he ate stars with sago. Koko was going around picking the stars and eating them when suddenly the tree shrank down to its original size. This was in the morning. Bapak Koko was still up there, but when the tree shrank, he fell into the water. When he fell, he dropped the stars and the sago. He looked at the river and ordered the salt water to go down to the sea and the sweet water to go upstream where he lived."

Asmat stories and myths do not follow any particular pattern. They do not have a beginning; they do not have an ending. They are usually difficult for Westerners to understand.

Nowadays, Paulus said, children are no longer interested in the old stories. They do not care to spend time in the men's house. They are learning new stories about Jesus. They are learning to play guitars that they make themselves and do not care to sing the old songs or listen to the drumming. They have not yet seen television, but soon will. The culture is already in transition. One day, it will all be gone.

2

Art and the Carvings

Asmat remains bewitching for me, in spite of the changes that began slowly and are now rapidly altering life. The Dutch military expeditions of 1906 to 1913 did little to establish any sense of peace for the Asmat, who were constantly at war with one another. Later, smaller expeditions, like those of Lord Moyne, Paul Wirz, and A. F. R. Wollaston, recognized the need for an understanding of the ritual carvings of Asmat and collected all they could, including information on the designs. It wasn't until Father Gerard Zegwaard began living in a village called Agats in 1953 that change became part of daily life. Agats turned into the administrative center of the colony, where the Dutch government set up a hospital and banned nudity in the town itself. Asmat men living around Agats quickly learned to wear shorts, and then long trousers and T-shirts. They discarded the bone and shell nosepieces that had given them a fierce, terrifying, exciting look. The women painted brassieres on their chests with a white paint that the men made from mussel shells, but did not completely reject the old style of body decoration. On occasion, a woman wearing a human jawbone as the centerpiece of a necklace can still be seen. The jawbone is discarded by the men during initiation ceremonies, after an enemy's head has been decapitated and left in the fire all night. It is literally thrown away. One of the women of the family retrieves the bone and wears it to show off the hunting ability of her husband.

Art and the Carvings

It is one of the great pleasures of my life to sit at the feet of a carver in Asmat, watch him work, and ask questions.

"What is that curled motif you are working on?"

"It is called *was wow*. It represents a clearing in the jungle, where the men sometimes meet to discuss warfare."

Among the carvers, there never was any such concept as artistic temperament. None of that, "Go away! Don't bother me! Can't you see I'm busy!" None of the attitudes of most artists in the West, the need to be alone to concentrate. In Asmat, it is rare, almost unheard of, to want to be alone. The carvers are carvers, no more, no less; that is what they are. They are not what we think of as Artists with a capital "A," who produce Art, with a capital "A." They produce artifacts to be used in rituals, carvings that embody the spirit of the dead ancestors for whom they are named.

When I am with the Asmat, I always have a sense of discovery about the carvings and about life itself. Everything is new to me, including watching a master carver work. Often, it is like sitting at the feet of a Buddhist master or Hindu saddhu. There is a feeling of being inside a temple surrounded by religious relics. Or it is like walking into one of the photographs taken by Frank Hurley of men's houses along the Gulf of Papua, taken in the early 1920s. The photos show a dark cathedral-like atmosphere, awesome enough to be Chartres itself.

That newness is true of daily life, too, as though I am entering a new world, which, indeed, I was, for my perception of everything around me changed. I was in another culture, one in which spirits floated through the men's house, through the family house, through the forest, ever-present in order to make sure that the rituals for the dead were being performed. Every cut in wood with knife of bamboo, shell, or steel used to produce a carving that embodies the spirit of an ancestor is one more step toward the appeasement of the dead, all of whom remain alert, awaiting their time to go on to Safan, doing evil, directing arrows and spears from targets of animals and birds, killing off the sago trees and all the fish of rivers and seas. Until the carving is complete and is being used in ritual life, the spirit is doomed to wander the earth.

The Asmat have no such word as "artist" in their vocabulary. Instead, there are descriptions: design man (*wow ipitsj*), clever man (*tsjestsju ipitsj*), man who carves well (*pamain aiptep*). There are other words, too, depending on the region of Asmat. In the same way, there is no word for "doctor" or "witch doctor." *Nadam bawor warumtau ipitsj* is a man expert at traditional medicine, and *iram ipitsj* is a spiritual man who makes magic. There is no actual payment for the services of a carver. I felt a kinship with them, for, like them, I was never in need of praise as a painter or writer. There was never any feeling of deficiency or insufficiency within

30

me. It was enough that I worked on occasion to make the money that allowed me to pay the rent, buy the groceries, and have the time to write or paint. I needed to unleash the forces that led me directly into what we of the West think of as creativity. I could identify with that calm and easy way most Asmat carvers have when producing their extraordinary work.

The carvers of Asmat, the carvers of New Guinea, the carvers of Melanesia, of most of Oceania, Africa, most of pre-Columbian Mesoamerica rarely thought of themselves as having a higher status than other members of the village. They were craftsmen. In Asmat, they were highly respected, their status equal to that of a revered headhunter, but it gave them few special privileges. Everyone knew who the best carvers were. When at work on a shield or a drum or an ancestor figure, the carver is relieved of the problem of feeding his family. He has no time to go into the forest to cut down sago palms for food. He does not go hunting or fishing. He works on a carving at his own pace. The commissioner of the artifact therefore takes on the responsibility of feeding the carver's entire family. He even brings special tidbits, such as tobacco or sago larvae, to keep him happy. This way of working, with the carver being commissioned, has almost disappeared.

All men, when carving—be it a paddle or an ancestor figure—have a placidity about them, an atmosphere of serenity in contrast to the violence of which they are capable. The calming aspect of the chisel in hand, carving designs in low or high relief, gives them a spirituality that communicates directly with the spirit forces necessary to their health and comfort.

This side effect of spirituality seemed to emanate from most carvers as I watched them work, particularly Ndocemen, my adoptive father, of the village of Sjuru. It was he who gave me his own father's name, Sembet. His capacity for violence was always to be seen, bubbling up like lava, always ready to explode, frightening me at times. He had a mean look about him that vanished only when he was working on a carving, even though he was not a master carver. Like most men, he worked on his own spears, bows and arrows, and paddles, unless they were to be decorated with incised head-hunting symbols. The lines of cruelty on his face relaxed, filled in, and faded away, giving him a whole other look, one of gentleness and peace.

All good carvers, even today, have one essential quality that always astonishes me: that of seeing a work clearly before beginning to carve. It is akin to Michelangelo saying, when faced with a block of marble, "The sculpture is there inside. I have only to chip away the outer layer."

On the Sepik River of Papua New Guinea some years ago, I watched a man incising a piece of pottery. The pot had been thrown by a woman; the man would decorate it. The pot rested in the hollow of his left hand. He

31

looked at it, turned it this way, turned it that way, imprinting its shape on his eye and brain. I was surprised at the intensity of his stare. It was clear that he was visualizing the entire surface of the pot in the round. He picked up an obviously beloved wooden stylus and warmed it in his right hand. He arranged the tool, turning it to suit the design, and proceeded to work. Somehow, he had divided the pot into four sections in his head. He started at the first section, went on to the second, continued at the third, and, finally, finished with all the sections equal, completely balanced, as though he had measured them. He did not lay out the design or sketch it onto the pot to make sure that each quadrant would be of equal length. He did not make a mark on one side, another on the opposite side, and then divide the two parts in half, as we might have done. He simply incised the pot without a moment's hesitation, going from beginning to end without a stop.

In the same way, the Asmat carver begins carving with his ax, blocking out several figures, one above the other, with swift, sure strokes, and then refining the whole with a nail chisel.

The Asmat work vertically, beginning at the top when roughing out the work and returning to the top when starting to refine the piece. The carving is usually held between the carver's legs while he is working on it, unless it is a large piece. It might then be put flat on the floor. All carvings are made from a single log or tree trunk. Figures and symbols are carved one above the other. Two pieces are never put together with nails or with the string made from the inner bark of the paper mulberry tree rolled on the thigh or sole of the foot. Even elaborately carved canoe prows, chiseled with ancestral symbols, were almost never added to the stem but were carved from a single piece. In certain villages, such as Jamasj and Jeni, prowheads sometimes were carved separately from the canoe they would adorn. They were tied onto the canoe when going into battle and then were removed to avoid accidental breakage.

It was essential to my work that I have a good relationship with various carvers and that we have the kind of rapport that allows for an easy flow of information. It was the older carvers who knew the meaning behind the symbols and the use of artifacts in rituals. Young carvers rarely understood the significance of the motifs. Their tools had not yet become extensions of their hands or their mood, so the images they carved were without vitality, without the life that meant a spirit resided in them.

There were two men from Ayam with whom I liked to have discussions: David Dicim and Alo Sosokcemen. Both were surprisingly knowledgeable about carving and ritual life, although their village had stopped carving ceremonial objects years ago. David was probably in his early thirties when I saw him last. Alo was somewhere in his mid-twenties. David had moved permanently from Ayam to Agats to work in the bishop's office. He was leading a sedentary life there and grew more bulky every time I saw him. He was no longer going into the forest, no longer paddling his canoe to cut down sago trees, no longer doing the physical work that had kept him trim. Being fat, of course, meant that he was affluent. He could pay for his food with cash in hand. Alo (whose last named translates as "black penis") was headman of Ayam. He had the usual Asmat men's well-defined muscles in chest and abdomen and looked as though he worked out regularly. Almost all Asmat men have this marvelous shape. He was probably the youngest headman in the whole of Asmat.

David and Alo sometimes sat with me in the men's house in Ayam or in my own house in Agats while I asked questions of the older carvers. In this way, they too learned. They were not carvers, but simply wanted to understand their own culture. They realized that it would not be long before the Asmat way of life disappeared. Both of them could interpret many of the symbols used in their own areas. They were quicker to answer questions than most Asmat and had been to the Catholic high school in Jayapura, capital of Irian Jaya, sent there with the financial help of the bishop.

They obviously liked sitting with me when I was with a master carver and never interrupted, never asked their own questions. They were absorbing information themselves. I learned the Asmat terms for almost everything connected with rituals, feasts, and carving, but the conversations were held in Indonesian (even though the older men were usually limited in their understanding of it), with the young men interpreting for me when necessary. All Asmat men, women, and children speak Asmat of one dialect or another. Most now speak Indonesian as well.

In these later years, when I take small groups of travelers around Asmat once or twice a year or when I am with larger groups on cruise ships, it is not possible to do research. Occasionally, certain questions may be asked, but when outsiders are around, carvers are generally reluctant to reveal information that they consider to be personal and secret. Gathering information was best when I was alone with the older men. Most of the Catholic missionaries were also interested in the culture, but the Asmat were reluctant to talk of their sexual lives and of warfare when they were around. When the Asmat were too shy or embarrassed to answer questions about head-hunting and cannibalism, I took them back into their own past, giving them a way out of answering directly by prefacing the questions: "In former times, before you were born . . ." Even when their own sons sat next to them, the carvers often closed up; the young are not thought to be ready to understand the essence of life in their carvings, just as young Jews are not thought capable of understanding the cabala.

Even now, after so much time in Asmat, after so many questions, I still have no translation of the word *ainor*. I have an interpretation, an explanation of it: I know that it is a head-hunting symbol; I know what it does and how it affects people. But what it actually means continues to elude me. Other symbols are easily understood. *Tar* is flying fox; *tarep*, feet of a flying fox. "Is it an animal?" I would ask. "Is it human? Is it a spirit? Is it something untranslatable that can only be called *ainor*? Does it provoke an image other than the one carved into the shield? Is it found on any other artifact?" No, they say, to all of these questions. Nor is there any word for it in Indonesian. The design is simple: two opposing spirals with a downward loop between them. It could be taken as a simplified form of two eyes and a nose. It is often confused with *bipane*, the shell-nosepiece motif that represents the tusks of a wild boar and is simply two spirals connected horizontally. The *ainor* is a common head-hunting symbol in at least two areas of Asmat. The *bipane*, in turn, is sometimes referred to as *fatsjep*, curled tail of a cuscus. I always had to remind myself that every village had its own myths, its own names for the motifs on the carvings. It often happened that even the two halves of a village would have different names for the same design.

If an enemy sees the *ainor* on a war shield, he immediately becomes immobilized and drops his weapons. A warrior can then capture him easily, tie him to a crosspiece in the canoe, and decapitate him at the bend of a river, where the spirits dwell.

Completely unaware during my first year in Asmat that my Western thinking was always getting in my way, I would ask, "Suppose your enemy has the same *ainor* on his shield that you do. What happens when you meet each other?" I was, of course, envisioning several possibilities, such as both warriors being immobilized, dropping their weapons, being captured by someone else, and later being decapitated in the canoe. The carver frowned, thought about it for a while, but showed only confusion on his face. "What are you talking about?" would seem to be written there, as though this kind of thinking, this kind of questioning, never appeared in Asmat culture.

Speculation is not part of Asmat thought processes. I can wonder to myself, or even ask a question aloud of a friend: Who first stood and watched the mating of praying mantises and saw the female devour the male immediately after copulation? Who had the curiosity, patience, and intelligence to stand and look, to analyze and decide that the praying mantis must be a head-hunting symbol? Who or what first led the carver's hand to the chisel to carve an ancestor pole? What induced a man in the Pyrenees to scrape his fingers over the soft limestone walls of the caves of Lascaux, Peche-Merle, or Altamira and thereby produce what may have been the first drawing there? Who, for that matter, first learned to cut down a sago palm, open the bark, pound the pith, pour water over it, squeeze out the liquid, allow it to settle and harden, and then roast it on the embers of a fire? It is a complicated and time-consuming process. Such unanswerable questions never appear to trouble the Asmat. They are more interested in daily life: When are we going into the jungle to pound sago? When is it time to hunt wild boar? When do we start making a new canoe?

It took me a long time to understand that life in Asmat, as lived on a daily basis, is fundamental and practical. The need for food and, in the past, the need for vengeance were of paramount importance. The forest was filled with sago, and the rivers were filled with fish and animal life; a family need only gather sago or go hunting or fishing. The demand by ancestors to avenge their deaths forced the Asmat to take others' lives to keep the cosmos in balance. Reciprocity and symmetry were necessary and were reflected in the use of carvings in ceremonies, the medium through which the living communicated with the dead.

Throughout my time in Asmat, I was welcomed everywhere in great style, not only by the carvers, but by all the men. The women rarely approached me; they were too shy, except during feasts when it was possible to join them in dance. There was always a physical and emotional distance between us. Invariably, there would be drumming and dancing in the men's house. Invariably, I would put out tobacco for the men and demand that they call the women to get their fair share. The next day, superb carvings would be brought out in the expectation that I would buy them. I bought for the museum in Agats and occasionally for the Crosier Museum in Hastings, Nebraska, as well as for friends of the bishop. It was under the bishop that I worked. At first, I traded with steel axes, machetes, fishhooks, nylon fishing lines, and other tools, but later, when the people began to understand money, I gave them hard cash.

Many of the carvings literally thrilled me. I look at them and feel their extraordinary power and beauty. Even to me, the carvings evoke the spirits of the dead for whom they are named. They call up a spirituality and a sensuousness that exudes an aura that goes deeply through the body of the carver. I can visualize the Asmat manner of working in wood: first hacking away with a steel ax into what would become an ancestor pole, and then refining and naming a spiritual piece when it was done. It was like an Asmat man with a pregnant wife finishing a fetus through the refinement of his sexual movements, his penis the tool that shapes the actual fetus's body. The man might roughly penetrate his wife, but in subsequent couplings would refine his activities by changing position during sexual encounters. He might move the direction of his tool from the right side to the left, from an upward motion to a downward one. The movements would become more and more subtle. This would assure both the man and the woman that the two halves of the fetus would be equally strong. They both would move again and again, further guaranteeing the child his or her complete health with balanced limbs: two arms, two legs, ten fingers, ten toes. The Asmat love their children.

Much as I enjoyed traveling around Asmat and doing research, I sometimes preferred staying in Agats, working at the museum. I would sit just inside the doorway of the storage room, so I could see whoever came through the door. It was one of my jobs to catalog the museum's entire collection. I had to determine the origin of all 1,000 pieces that were left after I had eliminated those of inferior quality, to learn the meaning of the symbols and their use in specific feasts, and to make sure that the museum had at least one example of every type of traditional artifact. I also collected modern pieces and set up displays with the help of Eric. I traveled widely, for there was no one in Agats other than David and Alo with more than superficial knowledge of the artifacts. In this way, I became familiar with almost every village in Asmat.

I was disturbed by the new carvings. For me, they had no spiritual relationship to those made before outsiders came to influence the style and finish of the artifacts. It is possible that if the carvers had changed through their own devices, the work would have continued its marvelous vigor and brawn. But under the influence of outsiders, the carvings were watered down and became artistic rather than art, amusing rather than exciting or beautiful.

I stayed longer in some villages than in others, depending on how forthcoming the carvers were in allowing me to watch them work and in providing information. I got to know people, had new names given me, and thoroughly enjoyed every minute of my time there. Of course, the Asmat watched what I bought and proceeded to make similar works for the next batch of travelers.

As the years went by, however, it became more and more obvious that change not only was inevitable, but had long since begun and was rapidly accelerating. It was also obvious that I was part of the change, was even one of the main media through which it was taking place. I had brought change simply by my presence; by wearing clothes; by bringing tobacco, steel axes, and knives as trade goods; by the very fact of my skin color. It is not possible for even one person to go to any remote region of this earth and not bring change.

After completing the card catalog in 1983, my work at the museum was ostensibly finished. Invitations suddenly appeared for me to lecture on Asmat on elegant cruise ships. This was hardly the same as living and working in Asmat, but it did enable me to return there on a regular basis.

The Asmat give wonderful receptions to groups of tourists, partly because they themselves have a good time and, more important, partly because they get paid to give travelers an exciting welcome. Some visitors complain about this payment: that the welcome is no longer the real thing, but is a staged performance. The fact is that payment of some kind is traditional. Asmat society is still based on reciprocity. If a man gives sago to his exchange, or *papisj*, partner today, the partner must give back to him something equivalent the next time he returns from the forest—pig meat, perhaps, or fish or sago worms. And each partner must help the other in all personal fights.

In the past, when arriving at a village, strangers presented gifts. For a long time, tobacco was the accepted offering. Now the people look for volleyballs, soccer balls, nets, school supplies, money. In exchange, receptions are as clamorous today as they were in the past. The idea of balance is central to Asmat life, central in the same way that the taking of heads used to be necessary to a stable universe.

The look of the Asmat, however, is now completely different from their former appearance. The most obvious difference is the clothing worn by both men and women. In the past, in the coastal regions, the men were naked except for the accessories of body decoration: nosepieces, necklaces, and dance belts that covered the buttocks but left the groin exposed. In the Balim Valley, where the Dani people live, penis sheathes are sometimes as long as two feet. Today, women who traditionally wear only a waistband called an *awer* are putting on brassieres when Westerners are around, brassieres bought in stores, woven from sago leaves, or painted on their chests, their nipples peeking through the white paint. The faces of the Asmat have a different aspect. The wild beauty is gone, or perhaps I can no longer see the former intensity of expression, their spontaneous, boisterous reactions, the reckless way they entered equally into battle and into frivolity, the self-assurance of their stance and stare, the look in those eyes reflecting pride. The whole manner of the men and women has changed, their posture, their attitude, now without the former easy flow of limbs. Clothing places restrictions on the body that did not exist in the past. It also is a great source of disease. Ringworm, for example, passed easily and quickly when someone wore the clothing of another member of the family.

Not long ago, I was invited on a walking trip with a tour group in the Jayawijaya Mountains, and then down to Asmat, traveling to several villages in the bishop's boat. The tour company paid the villagers well, and receptions were always astonishing. I was with the tourists when we had a series of noisy, extravagant welcomes everywhere. All eighteen of us—including Magnus, the tour leader, and me—were inside or on the roof of the bishop's boat coming in from the sea. We entered the Bow River on the way to Owus. Without warning, what seemed like hundreds of Asmat men were attacking us, screaming out their high-pitched yelps and terrifying many of the travelers. This reception was in the old tradition of attacking enemy canoes. The Asmat had been hiding behind the bend of the river and suddenly appeared as if to overwhelm us. The men were decorated with bone or shell nosepieces and necklaces; feathers in their hair; white, black, and red face paint; and feathered magic bags on their chests or backs. They were standing in their canoes, paddling, shouting, many of them swarming over our boat. The canoes lined up on both sides of us, maneuvered brilliantly to surround us, and changed formation again and again. It was a marvelous welcome.

As we approached Owus, we could see and hear the women, decorated like the men, dancing to drumming. They, too, were yelping. They threw various missiles—spears, arrows, branches—at the men in mock battle, a traditional aspect of most feasts and of a welcome into their village. The headman came up to Magnus and me. We were thanking him for the enthusiasm and excitement of the people when the headman said, "Well, then? Is that enough?"

I was astounded and completely deflated. Magnus's mouth fell open. "No!" he shouted, and the stimulation of the travelers continued as though nothing had happened. However, the headman's question left a pall over both Magnus and me. The changes taking place are coming too rapidly and are almost unbearable at times.

How could it be any other way? Most often, travelers are taken to the area closest to Agats, to the same villages over and over again, sometimes twice in one week, although a year or two may pass before another group comes along. We ask the villagers to receive us—to perform, if you will—with real enthusiasm, with all the men and women decorated, dancing, yelling, shrieking. How can we expect the people to be full of energy and excitement and passion every time we come? Some villages attack one another because particular villages seem to be chosen for visitors more often than others.

There are changes everywhere, in feasts, in carvings, in a great part of the way of life. Feasts that normally take four or five months to complete are now reduced to a morning or an afternoon of drumming and dancing. The shrinking of time to almost nothing removes the spiritual element from feasts and carvings. The carvings no longer emit the otherworldly quality that made them so remarkable. That is not to say that there are no spiritually invested works being made today. On the rare occasions when traditional feasts are held, the artifacts are as good and as evocative as anything in the past. This has nothing to do with the carvings made purely for sale, many of which have a more refined aspect than traditional works, but emit no spirituality whatsoever. Twenty years from now, however, the new carvings may begin to look like Art. I doubt it.

3

Marriage

I often mix my two friends together and am never sure whether it is Douglas or Aipit who sleeps on the mat next to mine, whether or not the mosquito nets are in place. I do not understand how this happened, how it is possible for me to live so comfortably, so fulfilled, in so remote a region of my sensibilities, my body, my brain.

I had formed a relationship with Aipit. I do not know whether he is still alive. I know only that he looked ill when last we met several years ago. His village is some distance from Agats, There is no radio, no telephone, no way to communicate with Aipit's village other than by chartering a canoe and going down there. A priest might stop there once or twice a year. Our connection was not an intellectual one, although our discussions were concerned primarily with the culture of Asmat.

Aipit did not understand the extent to which I was involved there, the why of my feeling so deeply about him and his people. We had no formal relationship, although at times I felt that we were *mbai* ritual partners, a kinship that in truth could not exist. I could no more be his true *mbai* than he could be my monogamous lover. I had no way of balancing our traditional relationship with his traditional reality. He knew this even better than I did.

I was always excited by the idea of a trip to Aipit's village in the bishop's mappi or outboard. Arrival at the edge of the sea was to arrive at some long-dreamed-of destination, one not on any map, the sea and land indistinguishable from each other, not an illusion, but wholly of the imagination, the sea dead calm, the flats of mud like quicksand as I stepped out of the boat, sinking deeply, almost prepared to be swallowed up.

In another land, Douglas and I, in a weak and dream-like moment of our own, formalized at least one aspect of who we were to each other. We were, in fact, married on a bench in the park in front of the building in which he lived on the east side of First Avenue and Second Street. He had taken ecstasy, a hallucinogenic and was very high. Even so, I had not expected the ritual that took place there.

From somewhere on his person, Douglas took out what might have been a small key ring, put it on the appropriate finger of my left hand, and said, "With this ring, I thee wed." I wasn't sure that I was hearing him properly. Then, "I love you and will always love you." I took the ring off and put it on *his* finger. I repeated his words, "With this ring, I thee wed." It was one o'clock in the morning, maybe later. I shook myself to make sure this was real and that I was awake. We held hands, we hugged. I didn't know if I was floating or sinking.

Do you have any idea what that meant to me? Have you any idea what it is like to have a young person pay close attention to you when you are old? I was discovering new worlds not only in the physical landscape and people around me, but through exploring the new worlds inside myself.

Soon, it began to get light. The sun was shining on the windows across the street, in my old building: 39 First Avenue. We went back to Douglas's apartment, which was empty of all guests but João, who was in John's bedroom. Both were dancer friends of Douglas's. The place was littered with plastic glasses and bottles, plus the usual paper plates with leftover pieces of pizza everywhere, on tables, on chairs, on floors, on beds. When Douglas was in New York recently, he read these pages and insisted that I was wrong about returning to his apartment. It never happened, he said.

The wedding ceremony had been simple, as uncomplicated as any marriage in Asmat, where the bride goes to the house of the groom, bakes sago, offers it to the groom, and that's that, the entire ceremony. It is all as simple and as matter-of-fact as the service on the park bench. Douglas and I never discussed this later; I assumed that he, having been in the hallucinatory world of ecstasy, had forgotten all about it. For me, the ring was real; the ceremony was real. I had been relatively sober after two vodkas and could remember all that had happened.

Douglas and I had met at a small dinner party at the apartment of mutual friends. Early in the evening, I had a chance to ask the usual questions: What do you do? Where are you from? When he answered that he was from New Zealand, I jumped: "Have you ever heard of a writer named Janet Frame?" It turned out that Janet Frame was one of his favorite writers. He could quote page after page of her poems, pages from her auto-biography and her fiction. He was delighted. When I told him that Janet and I were friends, that we had met at Yaddo and had spent a month together during a winter season, he immediately invited me to a rehearsal of a dance program he was choreographing in which he, among others, would dance. Janet was the bond that brought us together as friends.

If you knew Douglas, you would be just as surprised as I was at any kind of marriage ritual, however limited. It wasn't his style, but I was pleased and happy—even with a key ring. Nonetheless, it was difficult to believe what was going on. I had never considered it possible for anyone to fall in love with me or even to love me, let alone someone as remarkable as Douglas. He was not one to commit himself to anyone or anything but his dancing, which was his life. He loved men and women and loved them deeply, but it was the world of dance that filled his soul. I am not much to look at and am an old man. Douglas was in his twenties when we met. I was probably sixty-three or sixty-four. I thought carefully at first about our age difference and decided that it was best to forget about it. It didn't seem to matter whether the friendship would be long-lasting. Whatever pleasures were to be attained were enough. Whatever suffering might come upon me later would have been worth it. And so it was.

In Asmat, thoughts of age differences never come up. When I asked Aipit which of his two wives was the more beautiful, he said, "The older one." She was discernibly older by several years. "Why is that?" I asked. "Oh," he said, "she makes the best sago." She not only was older than the second wife, but was older than Aipit.

Douglas and his dancers had given the final performance of their gig at the Field, a dance space on Houston Street, that wedding night. He threw a party for members of his company and their friends, inviting me as a dancer. The ecstasy made him feel claustrophobic. He had to get out of his apartment, he said, but he didn't want to be alone. He asked me to stay with him, to protect him. He was loving and affectionate, and I forgot all about his Puerto Rican boyfriend, a source of jealousy on my part. Presumably, I was the intellect; the Puerto Rican of the big cock, the sex object. I was not what he was looking for sexually.

I, too, was high on the evening. The joy of performing, even in a minor role, was exciting for me. That night, after all, had been my dance debut, and I was making it in New York at the age of sixty-five. I was not a dancer, had never trained as a dancer, and had no pretensions as such. But Douglas and I did perform a pas de deux called *Dog Dance*.

The truth of the matter is that I didn't do much but walk around, mostly in slow motion, while Douglas danced his own choreography. I had to know all his movements as well as my own so I could coordinate what

I was doing with what he was doing. I had to be in the right place at the right time. It wasn't as easy as Douglas insisted it would be. He could visualize the dance as a whole, follow it through from beginning to end. He could see every movement clearly, every step. It was all in his head. Dance had been the major part of his life for fifteen years or more.

Unlike Douglas, I could not keep the images or sequence of movements in my head. I needed notes of some kind on paper. Once I had written them down, I had no trouble with the choreography and could follow the whole of the dance. The next year, I was in another performance with Douglas. It all went down on paper: bend, slap thighs, right foot out, slap head, slap arms at elbows, right leg up to left knee, slap foot, slap head with right hand. It was easy enough.

Douglas was dancing with the Paul Taylor Dance Company at the time. He was glorious on stage. His body moved with a grace that was heart-stopping. The audience at Paul's work *Arden Court,* in particular, couldn't get enough of the sensuous duet he performed with Christopher Gillis, wonderfully danced by both of them, with that little wiggle of the hip they both did so erotically.

In 1987, Paul asked three of his male dancers, including Douglas, to choreograph a five-minute work. It was the first time Paul allowed the work of any other choreographer to appear on one of his programs. Douglas made a piece called *Faun Variations,* variations on Nijinski's *Afternoon of a Faun.* This time, the music was Ravel's *Tombeau de Couperin.* Douglas's Faun was so astonishing and erotic that I could easily believe that he was a reincarnation of Nijinski. Being with Douglas and other performers, watching the dances come together, going backstage, learning a new language was another world for me.

Douglas was determined to form his own troupe with his own choreography. When he felt the urge, while he was still dancing with Paul, he pulled together a small group of dancers and choreographed new pieces for them. In time, a limited number of performances were given at the Field on Houston Street or at the "Y" on Fourteenth Street.

An offer came from the Arts Council of New Zealand, asking Douglas to return to New Zealand to start a company with grant money provided by the council. He was understandably of two minds about leaving New York, but I advised him to go. He would be a star there. New York was too full of small dance companies trying to make it, with too little money available. When he left that year, an empty space appeared in my life.

Douglas found something in me that he needed. I do not pretend to understand what it was, just as I did not understand what Aipit saw in me. It wouldn't have been difficult for Douglas to find someone more attractive or more affluent than I. It is easy enough to say that he was searching for a father or perhaps a grandfather, but it was more than that. Perhaps a bit of calm and sanity, a bit of warmth, affection, and love without demands. He always said I gave him self-confidence, especially about the dances he was creating. He admired me and I admired him, not only for his dancing but for his real intelligence and his ability to read rapidly and accurately and then retain it all. He read voraciously, his mind always absorbing immense amounts of material. He is curiously handsome, not with perfect features, but their configuration is such that they trigger something exciting in me. He is white-skinned, with blond hair and a short nose. He has a gymnast's body, tight and hard and muscular, a dancer's body, too; after all, he had started out life as an athlete. Sometimes, I look at him naked and wonder how this could have happened to me, how I could have been so accepted by him.

At times, he suffered agonies of anxiety attacks. He would call in the middle of the night, and I would take a cab across town to his apartment. I calmed him as best I could. I gave him Valium and got into bed with him. Under the quilt, he shivered. I hugged him tightly, repeating again and again, "It's all right. It's all right. I'm here." After an hour or so, he settled into sleep and I went home. He was fine in the morning.

There was something spiritual about Douglas. He had a transcendental quality that made him awesome when alone on stage. He exuded a combination of the sacred and the profane that, at least in my eyes, was ineffable.

Now, when I think of him, which is often, I juxtapose him with Aipit. I see them both clearly at the moment, although I know that memory distorts. There is nothing physically or mentally similar in them, only that there is something clean and beatific there.

I visualize Aipit within my mosquito net, sitting on my sleeping mat. We are alone in the teacher's house in Aipit's village. The teacher has gone into the jungle with his family to pound sago and won't be back for several days. Aipit's face is barely lit by the embers of the fire. He emits an ethereal, spirit-like atmosphere. His wives and children are a hundred feet away, sleeping contentedly in the family house, knowing that Aipit is with me. I see myself lying there, his eyes on me. We are naked. He bends down and stretches out on top of me. I feel comfortable there, satisfied, my stomach full, a great sense of calm and serenity enveloping me. We fall asleep.

I am in a land of spirits and spirituality. I can look through Aipit, through to the other side, and see all the generations of his ancestors, each one a headhunter, each one a cannibal. Aipit, too, has been a cannibal. Douglas is also on that other side. He moves forward and blends with Aipit. A light explodes from them, and they split and separate, each with his own luminous energy radiating around him. Each in his own way has given me a sense of creativity, the ability to express myself easily, freely. Each has shown me a new way, Aipit with his laid-back manner of coitus between men, the family accepting it completely, even delighting in the arrangement, and Douglas with his intense, incisive understanding of life.

In the past, those in Aipit's family who recently had died demanded vengeance so they might go on to the Land of the Dead. But Aipit is no longer disturbed by this, no longer terrified that the ancestors will wreak their own form of vengeance on him and destroy all the fish in the rivers and cause the stands of sago to rot. He is Catholic now and has been absolved by Jesus through one of the missionaries of the need to avenge the deaths of family members. He paddles into the jungle now, unafraid of attacks by men of other villages.

Aipit is as different physically from Douglas as a human being can be. He is dark-skinned, not a true black in color but a deep brown. He is Papuan, with kinky hair. He is tall for an Asmat, perhaps five feet, nine inches. Like Douglas, though, he has a superb upper body, developed through paddling his canoe every day. Unlike Douglas, he has relatively thin legs, since there is hardly any walking to be done in the Asmat forest. Douglas's thighs are thick with muscle, as are his calves. The smell of Aipit, the smell of sago and fish and the mud of the river on him, is erotic to me. The feel of his skin, rough in spots, silken in others, is also erotic.

I do not know what it is about Aipit that first encouraged me to touch him. It might not have been anything more than what I thought was a look of invitation in his eye or the light shining on the scar of his upper lip that gave me the confidence to pursue him. We were alone in the teacher's house, facing each other, our knees touching. As usual, the family was in the jungle pounding sago. I reached over and put a hand on his knee. Aipit remained motionless for some minutes before he put a hand on top of mine. He rubbed my hand. I looked at the grin on his face and understood enough to realize that this is a man with whom I could fall in love. Something about him moved me deeply. I might have been inventing his history as I sat there. How does one make a pass at a headhunter, even if he no longer hunts heads? I can still feel the rough skin of his palm when he rubbed the back of mine. I leaned over and pressed my lips against his cheek. The voices of women returning from fishing trips came to me out of the early-evening sky. Aipit was laughing, amused, pleased.

I moved and pushed him down onto the floor. I cannot imagine what might have been going on in his head. Was he thinking that I was too aggressive? Who was master, who slave? Would a bamboo knife appear suddenly to decapitate me? Was I breaking important taboos? Would Aipit allow my ministrations and join in with equal ardor, or would he laugh and sneer? I could feel that he was already hard. I kissed his lips and felt him respond with the pressure of his arms around me. I thought of his stick toothbrush, made from the roughened end of a twig, and wondered whether he had used it that day. I put out my tongue and tried to enter his mouth. He resisted strongly. I gave it up for the moment. He was quick to come that first time. It wasn't long before he began to pace himself to my own rhythm and to accept the joys of extending contact and of mutual gratification.

Over the next year or so, I visited him on at least two occasions, always staying at the teacher's house. Our relationship pleased me and seemed to please Aipit. I still had no idea of what his feelings for me might be or of what his sexual limits were. Often, he did not stay long, half an hour or so. He was not in the least inhibited when it came to varying positions.

Aipit and I were lying beneath my mosquito net when the drumming started. We got up and climbed down the notched log of a ladder. Someone handed Aipit a drum. The ground was thick with mud. A dozen or more men stood in a tight circle. No moon was visible. It was too dark to recognize anyone. Four of the men had drums. They began to chant to its rhythm. The other men were dancing slowly, moving their knees in and out, imitating a cassowary, elbows and hands flapping like wings. The drums beat faster and faster. I danced, too, part of the troupe. Here there was no need for me to write down dance steps; it was all repetition, the same movement over and over. The drummers were in an inner circle. Later, I learned that the men were welcoming me back to their village. Douglas would have taken to Asmat dancing in an instant. Its very awkwardness would have challenged him.

I never stayed in Aipit's village for very long, a week or two at most, two or three times a year. The village was not easily reached. It is at the edge of the Arafura Sea, on the far side of which lies Australia. The houses are not more than 250 feet inland, on their own narrow river, the villagers' highway to the stands of sago and their fishing grounds.

Aipit gave me pleasure in many ways. He was entirely open about the sexual life of the area, denying that any ceremonial exchange of wives, *papisj,* still took place, but confirming that the full role of the *mbai* connection was still there—at least in that particular village, at that particular time. It was Aipit who first talked to me of these matters, the relationship between two men in the far south of Asmat. It was an affiliation based on reciprocity in many aspects of life. The men were ritual partners for life. Marriage between men and women could easily be dissolved, but there was no possibility of divorcing a *mbai.* Partners did not necessarily live in the same village. Now, most (if not all) of these pairings of two men are gone. Bonding between women does not appear to exist or to have existed in the past.

Marriage

I never learned how I fit into the scheme of things. I knew only that everything was out in the open about Aipit and me. I knew that he must have had a male partner close by. I worried about his possible jealousy and anger, but later I heard that important men often had more than one *mbai*. I accepted whatever came my way. The relationship was a comfortable one and was never thought of as either normal or abnormal by me or by Aipit or by anyone in his family. It was simply the way of life.

Aipit certainly did not love me in the Western sense of the word "love." Yet there was a fondness that went beyond pleasure in gifts. When he smiled and called me "*Mbai*" instead of using my name, I knew that there was something between us, even though I had not heard the word used as an endearment between men. He was covetous and at times even demanding. After all, we were *mbai* and were destined to share our wealth. Gifts to me came from all over the village—carvings, sago, shrimp, the skull of the ancestor for whom I was named.

One night, Aipit took me into his family house and indicated that I might have sex with the younger of his wives. This was a remarkable moment for me. It took me into the family; it took me into the whole structure of Asmat society. Under ordinary circumstances, I might have had any woman in Asmat. The people would have felt honored and pleased and would have expected to receive a number of gifts from me in exchange. However, this was different. The offering of Aipit's wife meant that I had gone beyond the barrier that separates cultures, that I, too, was a *mbai* and had all the privileges and obligations of the relationship.

The image of Aipit's younger wife is easily brought up, even now after the seventeen or eighteen years since I last saw her. We had never talked. When she gave me food, it was always through Aipit. She was even shyer than most Asmat women and kept her eyes down whenever we were in the same room. She was always silent.

Aipit's older wife was asleep at her own fireplace, a few feet away. The younger was still awake, lying on her back, her eyes closed. There were other family members around. The only light came from the glowing coals of the fireplace. The men were sleeping in the men's house. It was traditional for the major part of the family to sleep elsewhere whenever there was an exchange of wives.

The younger wife turned on her side. I was nervous and frightened of not being able to consummate the act. I leaned down and nestled into her body, my arm around her waist. She did not move. The smells that were erotic coming from Aipit were disturbing coming from his wife. I felt inadequate and could not perform. It had nothing to do with this beautiful woman, only with my own impotence with women in general. Aipit rubbed my shoulder with his hand. I looked into his calm, smiling face. He could not understand what was happening within me. Yet he did not seem upset; there was no anger in him. I moved away, and he took over my role, acting as my proxy. I wondered then and wonder now what they all thought. I spent the night in the family house without sleep, going over and over in my mind what I might have done. The next day, Aipit was his usual self. I imagined that the whole village knew of my failure, but there was no indication of it.

It was not only as a friend that Aipit gave me pleasure. The process of gathering information on the *mbai* relationship itself was equally exciting, partly because of the crowd that was eager to participate in answering questions. Males of all ages came to the teacher's house, from elders to youngsters of four and five. There was no hint of embarrassment on anyone's part. The children seemed to know all there was to know.

The pleasure of being with Aipit in the jungle was there, too. He wanted me to understand all that he understood. He was amused by my stupidity and my awkwardness. He laughed out loud when I inadvertently grabbed hold of a thorny vine to steady myself when trudging through the forest. He picked out the prickles from my palm and fingers. My clumsy ways made me laugh, too.

Aipit was aware of everything around him, as were all Asmat. They walked barefoot over thorns that went right through my sneakers into the soles of my feet. They had a tightrope walker's sense of balance, walking along the edge of the canoe as though they were on land. They understood every sound from the forest and could spot any movement within it. I knew nothing and could do nothing. Even the spoken language was difficult. They knew on which trees the birds of paradise mated. They knew how to trap the marsupial cuscus. They knew where to get fresh water in the midst of the saltwater tidal swamp. They were as intimate with the forest as I am with the New York subway system.

Aipit accepted me as a pupil, but it was slow work for him. Eventually, I learned to use my eyes to see crocodiles on the bank of the river before they disappeared into the water and to see the birds dancing in the tops of trees; I could listen and hear the same birds flapping their wings, calling to one another. I could hear the wind and listen to the talk that came along the surface of the river, as though by means of a telephone line.

I became aware of certain bird and animal calls that appeared at particular hours of the day. I began to understand the changing tide. Daily life connected itself to the whole environment. The Asmat were hunters and gatherers. They were dependent on only what the forest yielded and knew everything that was edible, everything that was useful. They were completely self-sufficient and needed nothing from the outside world until Westerners came to teach them other ways. Douglas, too, is self-sufficient now. He needs only a space in which to perform, and even that is not necessary. He can see the dances in his head.

So I had two teachers late in my life, Douglas and Aipit, both of whom added immeasurably to my understanding of myself and of the world around me. I cherish them both. I am wedded to them both.

4

The Sorcerers

I was sitting in Father Toon van de Wouw's house in Basim with four Asmat men: Betakam, Ndaise, Kaup, and Tete. I had asked Toon to invite these older men to talk about witchcraft and magic, prompted by information that I had gathered some months earlier. It is not a topic that normally crops up in conversation.

On the earlier visit, in July 1977, death by sorcery and its consequence had been explained to me by Florentin Wayet, one of the villagers of Basim. "When someone dies suddenly," he said, "not killed openly by an enemy, and not after a prolonged illness, but by a falling tree or a sudden drowning or a death without warning, the family gathers around the body to determine who performed the magic that killed him." Only old people and tiny children die of natural causes in Asmat; all others are killed by enemies through sorcery. These deaths, of both men and women, must be avenged by a killing, in order to put the cosmos back into balance.

The head of the family—often the father's eldest brother, sometimes the mother's eldest brother—asks questions of the dead person. With a spear with a cassowary claw at its sharpened end, he touches the forehead of the dead person, tapping it each time he asks a question. First the dead man is asked if he was killed by someone from another village. If the answer is yes, the body jerks violently and bounces up and down. Then the names of all the surrounding villages are called out, one after another, until the leader comes to the name of the offending village. The body then begins to jerk again, expressing anger and vengeful feelings. If the answer is no—that is, if the body remains in a quiescent state—the sorcerer asks, in turn, about each house in the dead man's village. If and when he comes to the right house, acknowledged by the twitching of the body, the question must be asked about each person in the house. If the answer continues to be no, the questioner goes on: "Did you eat any food that is taboo for you?" Then the family head lists the various foods that everyone knows had been forbidden to the dead man: "Did you eat cuscus meat? Did you eat shrimp?" When the right food is named, the body trembles and shakes. The men then stand up, knock their spears together above the body, and, in unison, give a great shout: "Whuh!" Everyone is happy. They all run to the river screaming, " It's all right! It is all right! Don't worry! He died from eating thorn fish!"

I had heard this story from Wayet when I was going from house to house while trading for artifacts and asking questions. This time, I was sitting in the pastor's house with four local middle-aged men who wore tattered shirts and shorts. All four were known sorcerers. There was nothing different about them, nothing magical or mysterious. Certainly there was no malevolence in their eyes. Although the look of the men was obviously Asmat, from the shape of their heads and bodies, they all had different facial features—except for the sameness of their huge noses, extended through a lifetime of wearing either shell or bone nosepieces.

In childhood, the septum of both boys and girls would be pierced with an arrow point, the hole enlarged first with sticks and then with shell. Nowadays, when head-hunting and warfare are almost nonexistent, only a few men and women wear nosepieces of any kind. Women wear them only during feasts. Children no longer undergo the piercing ritual. The shell nosepiece, the *bipane,* is made of two sections of the *Cymbium* shell cut into spiral form, tied together with rattan, and glued at the binding with beeswax or resin. The symbol resembles the tusks of the wild boar, which it is meant to imitate—a fierce, terrifying, and immensely strong animal, capable of ripping into the abdomen of a man and pulling out all his innards.

The *bipane* itself is one of the most important head-hunting symbols of Asmat. The bone nosepiece, called *otsj* or *firat,* is carved to represent the roots of a banyan tree, a tree in which women who die in childbirth are buried. Nowadays, when the need or desire to wear one arises, men and women might cut a nosepiece from a bucket made of plastic, preferably red, and tie it in place with string.

The four men in Father van de Wouw's living room chatted among themselves. They had no problem talking to one another, revealing long-hidden secrets that had been handed down from one generation to the next. In former times, they never would have talked this way outside the family. Even then, conferring together would have been in a secluded spot, away from anyone who might eavesdrop to learn the secrets. Times have changed since the days of cannibalism, when it meant taking in the strength of the man killed, along with his flesh. Most of the talk had been filtered through Ndaise, who was as articulate with his tongue as with his hands. He spoke excellent Indonesian, while the others were limited in speaking and understanding any language but Asmat. All four sat uncomfortably in chairs, cross-legged as though on the floor. They all had their heads shaved, like members of one family in which a close relative had just died.

Ndaise took the lead and began talking to us on his own, not waiting for one of us to ask questions. He spoke easily, softly, in traditional Asmat fashion, almost whispering. In more remote villages, men with secrets often spoke directly into my ear so that even spirits might not hear. The four men obviously had agreed to discuss the various antidotes to pain first. It all started calmly enough: "Now, we regularly have a lot of pain. Something or someone is always trying to harm us. Spirits are always around, turning over the canoe when we are out fishing or jabbing us with branches as we walk through the forest or covering us with angry thorns so large they enter the flesh on one side and come out the other. Spirits are always pestering us now that we are no longer killing for vengeance. There are good spirits, too. In fact, these very same spirits that turn over the canoe also help gather fish or they help when we are out in the jungle hunting wild boar or they keep the sago growing well. We must keep them content. They do not yet know that Jesus has absolved us of the need to take revenge on our enemies. They will learn."

I had placed a plug of tobacco on the low table around which we sat. Each of the men had brought strips of nipa leaf in which to roll the tobacco. They knew that they would get it from me. They had also brought a piece of the glowing firewood that they used instead of costly matches.

"But we were talking of pain," said Ndaise. "We have so many ways of lessening pain or of curing it. One way is with shredded *daure* fruit mixed with charcoal. First, we make small cuts next to one another in the skin over the area where the pain is most intense. Small cuts, you know, usually vertical rows, up and down, each row at an angle opposing the row next to it, making a fishbone pattern."

Ndaise carefully took off the feathered magic bag that he wore on his chest and from it removed a small mussel shell. He also took out an old stone that had been used as an ax, but now served primarily as a mallet when making carvings. He touched the stone tenderly, held it in one hand, and rubbed it with the other. He sat up straight and sniffed the air, as though waiting for the spirit within the stone to enter him through his nostrils. He broke the shell with the stone and picked up one of the smaller pieces. He held it out to us: "The cuts are made with a bit of shell just like this. It is like cutting a man's calves when making the glue to seal the lizard skin to the top of a drum. The cuts are made with a bit of shell; the blood wells up, flows out, and is caught in other shells, three or four of them. The blood dries out quickly and coagulates. You can almost see the *ndamup* spirit wiggling there, waiting to get back into the body of the man whose blood had been taken. It makes a glue when mixed with white lime and, far to the southeast of Asmat, human sperm. The sperm, the Marind people say, seals the ancestral spirit inside.

"The shredded fruit is then rubbed onto the cuts, where the pain lives. The scars are the *kiki* we all have on our arms and thighs, on our chest and back, that protect us from all kinds of magic. I always carve the *kiki* in the right places. See here? On the back of my thigh? A tree fell on me while I was sleeping in the bivouac. My father cut those marks there when I was in so much pain, I could hardly walk. After he made the cuts, there was no pain."

It sounded sensible to me, at that moment. Why, as a child, was I never cut in similar fashion to relieve pain? Didn't Western doctors bleed their patients at times not so long ago? My mother said that she had used a piece of raw potato to draw out the bad blood from a cancerous growth she had had on the side of her nose. It seemed to work. The cancer disappeared, but turned up later on another part of her face. Was that different from using shredded leaves? The cuts might have worked on me even had I not been conscious of the reasons for them. In Asmat, I had been scarified to give me speed and strength, cut with a mussel shell on my shoulders. I had accepted that. I could accept a release from pain, as well.

During initiation ceremonies for both boys and girls in Basim, I saw small circular burns, or *tumenes,* being made with the fiery end of a burning stick, a double row of them on each arm, from wrist to shoulder, the flesh sizzling each time the stick was pressed into it. The young did not cry out when this was done. They seemed to be able to bear the pain of one burn after another without flinching. They believe in the spirits. The young and the old live their whole lives with spirits ever-present around and among them. The spirits help them, those within as well as those of their ancestors. They are there, easing the way, giving them courage.

Burns like the *tumenes* may also be a specific for tooth pains and for pain in areas of the body where the cutting method does not work. The burns are made as close to the place of pain as possible. Some men and women are afraid of the burns and prefer the skin-cutting method; others fear the cuts and prefer the burns.

The Sorcerers

There are cures for lung pains, for chest pains, for eye problems, and for most difficulties, including potions for inducing love in another person. Men who are known for their particularly strong magic are called *orumpit;* women are known as *orumtawot.* A man or a woman may be called in to cure an illness, depending on who performed the magic that caused the illness. The sick person shows the sorcerer the location of the pain. The sorcerer then makes the cuts or burns. The more powerful the illness, the deeper the cuts; the deeper the cuts, the more blood must flow. The cuts and burns force out the bad blood, thus relieving the pain. If the victim recovers, he or she goes into the river to bathe. But the victim, often in agony and too weak to eat, may consume nothing for days, weeks, even months. In this way, he or she eventually dies of starvation.

Formulas for curing certain illnesses are most often inherited from someone in the family. To ensure the continuation of a particular line of sorcerers, more than one person is instructed. Each family has special prescriptions of its own. These formulas remain within the family and are transmitted by one male member to another male, one female to another female. A father teaches his eldest son, who may teach a younger brother.

Kaup had been silent during most of this talk. He was the only one of the four who was bare-chested. He felt closer to the spirits when he was completely naked, when the spirits could enter him through his uncovered skin. Like Ndaise, he was a carver. Both Ndaise and Kaup specialized in making remarkable drums with head-hunting symbols and animals carved into the handle and in relief on the body of the drum. Both also carved elaborate prowheads. Kaup's carved relief works were probably more interesting than those of Ndaise. He usually kept his head clean-shaven. Ndaise and Kaup appeared to have a lot to contribute at that moment. Ndaise wore a hat. I had not met with the other men before. They talked to Ndaise and to Kaup, but not directly to us. They were shy, turned in on themselves.

"Take a small red fruit called *tufe,*" said Kaup. "The fruit must be from a tree that grows on the bank of the river, not from a tree of the forest. That will be of no use. Next, take a *kamak* leaf and cut it into small pieces with a bamboo knife." Kaup gestured as though he had the fruit and the leaves in his hands. "You must be careful here," he went on. "Only a bamboo knife may be used, not a metal one and not one of shell. Mix the fruit and the leaves together and wrap it all in nipa leaves and rub it with only a special stone, one kept only for this purpose. The stone is not to be used for sharpening knives. It came down from the mountains a long time go, with our ancestors. It is called *eke.* It is light gray in color and is shaped like a *tufe* fruit." The sorcerer picked up the *eke* and faked throwing it at his victim. "He stands within sight of the victim and does this many times. He throws it and he throws it, asking the spirit of the stone to fly out and strike the victim."

Kaup stood up and demonstrated how to throw the stone without throwing it. The movement was like that of throwing a baseball, but there was something almost mystical in the way he used his arm, as though he were doing tai chi or chi kung, as though he were entering another world in which he floated and moved in slow motion.

"Now," he said quietly, "take up the bundle of chopped leaves and put it in the fire." I could feel that Kaup was in some way transporting himself into another place, another mental state in which his magic, whether from the leaves or from his own spiritual energy, would make that particular moment as real as the moment he had last performed this very rite.

"After a while, take it out and stuff the ashes inside three claws of a cassowary's foot. Put the claws on the first three fingers: the thumb, the forefinger, and the middle finger. The sorcerer points the three fingers at the quarry at the hottest time of day, never during cloudy weather.

"While pointing the fingers, many spirits will fight against him." Kaup pointed his own three fingers at an imaginary victim and then began waving his arms in the air. "Yes," he said, "some spirits will fight him; other spirits will help him. Sometimes, this fight is so terrible, the sorcerer faints and remains unconscious for three or four hours. If the magic is powerful enough, it will be working truly by then.

"The sorcerer always takes precautions before beginning to perform any kind of magic. If by chance, someone sees the sorcerer pointing, the victim can erase the effect of the magic by appointing a sorcerer to counteract it. In this way, there may be no pain, no death."

Kaup described all this as though haunted by memories that surfaced, receded, surfaced again. There were moments when his words were mechanically spoken from a time when he might have been reciting memorized lines learned in the men's house. Listening to that monotonous voice, it was easy to float off into another world, as though the day were gone or just beginning and I was an integral part of the sorcery and was, in fact, a sorcerer myself. At times, Kaup seemed to be holding himself in, perhaps fearful of spirits that might harm him for talking of these matters to outsiders. At other times, he appeared to have entranced himself, to have taken himself off into the spirit world itself.

I broke into the monologue, partly to break the spell and bring him back into the pastor's house, and partly because I wanted to hear what the other men had to say on other subjects: headaches and their cures, and matters related to death.

"Many Asmat, far upstream," I said, "tie a length of rattan around the head when they have a bad headache. They pull the rattan as tightly as possible until the headache goes away. Do you do that here?"

"*Tidak,*" they all said, shaking their heads. "No, but we have not heard of that cure. Here, we just make the cuts in the forehead."

"There was another method on the Brazza River," I added. "When the head hurts badly, the men pull tufts of hair as hard as they can. That is, a man will tell his brother-in-law about the pain, and the brother-in-law will gather a small bunch of hair in his fingers and pull on it, hard. Then he takes some of the hair next to it and pulls again, as hard as he can. This goes on all around the head. I have watched this performance from morning until evening, with one man having his hair pulled to ease the pain."

"*Tidak, Tidak,*" they all said again. "We have never heard of that cure. It does sound good."

I agreed that it was a time-consuming method and perhaps not truly efficacious. I changed the subject: "You were talking before about the *eke* stone and the sorcerer making believe that he was throwing the stone at his victim, to kill him, or to make him violently ill. I heard something like that in Atsj from Finasius Uwi. It was not the same, but one reminds me of the other because of the spirits involved.

"I had bought an *amosus* from Finasius. It had been carved by his father, Ewumber. It is very small and looks like a miniature sago pounder. Finasius told me it was used by the war chief to pull the enemy toward him. The war chief goes as close as he can to the enemy and calls out in a loud voice, '*Djot po! Bayu po! Badji now tsjes!*' In the dialect of Atsj, it means, more or less, 'Come on! Come on! Row to us like crazy!'"

"Oh! Oh!" said the four men. "The people of Atsj are the real headhunters and cannibals. We of Basim were never like that."

"The *amosus,*" I resumed, "was held out the full length of an arm and pulled to the body, drawing in the enemy. Sometimes, before attacking, while still in the village, while still in the men's house, where all the men were fully decorated and were drumming and dancing, the war chief would call out, '*Ndei.* Come. Amanamkai!' He would be using the *amosus* to draw them in to where the people of Atsj could surround and attack them."

As I was talking, recounting a story that had been told to me in vivid detail in Atsj, I found myself falling into the sorcery that I was describing. I had believed implicitly in the truth and reality of the Atsj chief's story and was changing roles with him as sorcerer. I fell into the cadence of his speech, fell into the manner of his movement, felt the approach of Kaimo's canoe, watched the men paddling in unison, their eyes staring blankly as I pulled on the *amosus.* "*Ndei!* Amanamkai! *Ndei,* Kaimo!" I whispered, while gesturing as the war chief had done. "Come, Kaimo!" I easily entered that necromantic world with the men of Basim around me, easily fell into the supernatural aura that was enveloping us all.

"Sometimes," I went on, "when out fishing, the chief and his family would happen upon people pounding sago and he would call out to them, 'Come to us, people of Omandesep, so we can kill and eat you. Come to us!'" I became the war chief, making the magic that would bring the enemy closer. "Come, so we can kill you!" I called to them. "Come, so we can eat you, just as we of Atsj have already eaten so many of Asmat. Come!"

Asking directly about death and vengeance was difficult. Traditional head-hunting in Basim and the South Casuarina coast almost certainly was never practiced as frequently and devastatingly as it had been only a few miles to the north in Atsj and Otsjenep. Enemy heads were taken when the opportunity and need arose. It is a subject that the men were reluctant to discuss partly because the pastor was with us. Father van de Wouw was trusted by members of his parish and was sympathetic to them, but there were occasional happenings about which the people were shy, fearing some spiritual retaliation. We were already in a deeply metaphysical mood, and I was not sure where we were going. My journal was open in my lap, and I was writing without realizing what I was doing. My mind kept fogging up, clearing for some seconds, then fogging up again.

When Tete's wife died in childbirth some months earlier, he carved a large horn from a *tu* tree. He blew the horn every evening to make all the pregnant women of the village die. He was angry about his wife's death, angry about the death of the baby. He wanted to kill all the women who were pregnant. Most of those in Basim got sick after hearing the horn, but none died. Tete's sorcery had not been powerful enough.

Tete had gone to the pastor when he saw that he must make a new horn immediately and blow the horn to save his wife's life. His anger and his need for vengeance, however, were not strong enough to kill so many women. First, the baby's hand came out. It was blue. The baby was already dead inside its mother. She had made the best sago and always had shrimp for him when he got up in the morning. Tete had her body carried around the village in a traditional procession.

She was wrapped in a mat of pandanus leaves and placed on a platform, as had been done in the days before the arrival of the pastor of Basim. A bow and arrows were placed on top of the mat, the arrows longer than the full length of the body. Women relatives were mourning the death. They crept along the side of the platform, moaning and wailing. They removed their groin coverings from around their waists and rolled around in the mud in order to keep the spirits from recognizing them. Recognition would lead the spirit of Tete's wife to try to enter another body and control it.

The Sorcerers

The bone of a male cassowary was put into the fire, taken out, and then pressed onto where the head was under the mat. The body was pointed in the direction of other villages. Tete asked it a series of questions in an angry voice: "Oh, why did you die? Why did you leave me? Tell me who it was who killed you. Was it someone from the village of Pirien? Someone from the village of Otsjenep? Was it someone from Japtambor?" Before each question, the body was turned slightly to face the specific village named. Finally, Tete demanded, "Was it someone from our own village of Basim?"

There was a pause somewhere in the atmosphere itself. The universe seemed to stop all movement, as though it were taking a breath. It was a fearful moment, and the silence was extraordinary. In some manner, I was transported into the middle of Tete's village. I could hear the birds in distant trees. I could hear the fish jumping in the river. I could hear the mudskippers racing along the surface of the mud and plopping into the water. Then, without warning, the bow and arrows began to shake and to make terrible noises. The killer was someone in their own village! It was someone they all knew! With those sounds of the rattling bow and arrows, it was obvious that the source of the death of Tete's wife was someone in Basim itself. The body and the bone were pointed in the direction of one of the houses. "Is this the house where the killer lives?" demanded Tete. The body was turned toward another house, and the question was asked again. Then another house and another until they were in front of the house of Tete's family, the house in which the killer lived. The arrows flashed and flew around in a whirlwind on top of the mat in which the body of Tete's wife was wrapped.

The moment came when Tete was pointing the bone in every direction. He pointed it at his father, at his own brothers-in-law, at each member of the family. The bow and arrows lay still. There was an unendurable silence. The bone and the body were moved again. "Is this the person who killed you?" Silence again. Then another movement of the body. The bone went into the body, and then onto the forehead of Tete's wife. Tete yelled out, "Is this the person who killed you? Tell us! Tell us! Is this the one who killed you?" I did not know what was happening right in front of my eyes.

It was as though the world were suddenly coming to an end, as though the cosmos were turning itself on end and whirling like a great spirit of cloud. At first it seemed that the arrows were murmuring to one another. They suddenly stood on end. They flew into the air, fought with one another, and knocked one another off the platform. They made frightening noises, like crustaceans from under the sea crackling the bones of a huge fish, like the creaking, mountainous rumblings of an earthquake.

The cassowary bone did not move. It lay perfectly still and was clear in

57

its direction, pointing toward a relative from the village of Omandesep who was staying with Tete's family. I was completely caught up in the spell of the story, in my own trance, side by side with the relative of Tete, watching the body as it was turned slowly, inch by inch, until it was pointing at me. It was my most terrifying moment, changing my concept of the world and of the universe.

Was I being hypnotized? Had I, unaware, been given some drug of which I knew nothing? I was seeing things that could not happen.

I felt the bone piercing my skin, piercing my flesh. The body lay still within the pandanus mat. Slowly the bone tilted upward. The point pierced the mat and seemed to penetrate the dead flesh within. The bone moved slightly and was directed at the man next to me. I began to shiver, and the man watching me begin to tremble violently, shaking his head, shrieking out words and unidentifiable sounds. Sometimes, there was no sound from him, and his screams could not be heard, even though his mouth was opened widely. He had begun to realize that it was he himself who had killed Tete's wife, that the cassowary bone was pointing directly at him, not at me, proving him to be the killer. He had not known that he had killed Tete's wife, that in fact it had been done by his *ndamup* spirit when it was out of his body. He turned and ran. He ran and ran. He entered the forest and was gone, disappearing, never to be seen again, never to be heard of again. He had been gathered up instantly by the spirits and taken to Safan, taken beyond where the sun sets, into the Land of the Dead, beyond the world, beyond vengeance, beyond redemption.

5

Walkabout

I have been on a walkabout all my life. My time in Asmat complements that in New York. The contrast is extreme; so different are they from each other that they might as well be on two different planets, as indeed they almost are.

In New York, I have friends I love: Floriano, Shirley, Dorle, Ed and Neil, Curt and Hortense, Claire, Sheila, Allan, Andrew, Claud, Rick, Berenice, Diana—a good list of people I see regularly and a much longer list of those I see less often but love nonetheless. It does not matter whether I see them once or twenty times a year, they are my friends. In Asmat, I have my Asmat friends—Ernes Dicim, Yuven Biakai, Aipit, Jeremias, Ben, Natalis—and I have my missionary friends: Al, Trenk (recently gone the way of all flesh), Jerry, Vince, Jim, and others in both categories. All these, in addition to those around the world, in Italy and England, Malaysia, New Zealand, Australia, in all six continents, including our own.

I am wonderfully lucky.

Now, I am again at Yaddo, an artists' retreat smack in the middle of New York State. It is impossible for me to be at Yaddo without thinking of David Vereano, whom I met here many years ago. He was young and handsome, a painter of landscapes with a sure eye and hand for color and form. His work was physically small, but it had greatness. An eight- by ten-inch painting expanded in imagination, for it had the feeling of immense size. The paintings were compact and full of life, so much so that the hillsides and valleys looked as though they were filled with painted people and animals. The greens and blues of his brushstrokes gave the illusion that there was a farmer actually plowing there and that his wife was somewhere near the barn feeding the chickens. The paintings were silent, never shouting to call attention to themselves; they gave out an aura of peace, gentleness, and gentility, just as he himself did.

It is also impossible for me to be at Yaddo and not think about Asmat. There are no real connections between them, only as memory makes its own associations, real and unreal. Some device I have not yet recognized connects them. Perhaps it is simply my sense of and need for aloneness in the forest, any forest, it does not matter. Is it the isolation from everyone and everything? Is it the gloom, the denseness of the growth, the smells of decaying leaves? Or is it simply the fact that each time I go to Yaddo, I take my slides of Asmat and at some point during my stay give a talk on the daily life. No matter, the connection is there.

The year David and I met, he was wearing a mustache, which gave him the appearance of a Levantine, which indeed he was, a Sephardic Jew born in Alexandria, Egypt. His nose was not Semitic, but his skin was swarthy and those huge dark eyes of doves came right out of the Song of Solomon, vital and searching, enriching him with everything those eyes captured and recorded. His gift lay not only in his paintings, but also in his ability to understand antiques. It did not matter what period he looked at, instinct and intelligence led him in the right direction and he had the additional strength of being able to act on impulse. He also had a warmth that enveloped everyone within his circle of friends. Both women and men fell in love with him, although only men physically attracted him. It was easy to open one's heart to David: he was so helpful and generous that even strangers immediately felt drawn to him.

David was assistant to Curtis Harnack, the director of Yaddo at the time. His job involved meeting new arrivals, escorting them to their bedrooms and to their studios, making sure they were properly settled, taking them on a tour of Yaddo, and showing them the great Tiffany glass windows in the mansion and the huge, individual portraits of Katrina and Spencer Trask and of their children. It was the Trasks who left Yaddo to artists of all kinds, a place where they could work without having to think of shopping, cooking, or the telephone. Even the portrait of Miss Pardee, nurse and governess to the children, was important in the context of Yaddo's life. David would talk about the history of the estate: West House; East House; the mansion; the various cabins in the woods; the graves of Katrina and the others buried in the Family Circle; Elizabeth Ames, the first director; her sister Marjorie Peabody Waite, who had been adopted by George Foster Peabody and who had suggested Elizabeth as director in the first place. Miss Pardee and George Peabody are also buried there.

David had it all down pat, showing the guests where the keys to the various buildings were hidden, giving them the schedule of mealtimes, and explaining all the rules and regulations that we adhere to with grace and understanding. He took an old storage room attached to the barn and made it into a studio for himself, which he called Archway. There is a sculptor in it now, Ron Baron. At first, I resented his occupying David's space, but other visual artists had been there after David had established himself in Durham, New York, and I had never thought to resent them. When I first reentered that studio at Ron's invitation, however, memories of David rushed at me, but they were good, fruitful memories, sad but not depressing. David's spirit is benign and sweet, balancing the force of the vibrations emanating from Ron and his work. David's laughter, too, remains to dispel any despondency.

David fell in love with young men with a fair amount of frequency and had many exciting affairs, although only two or three were seriously important to him. He went to bars in Albany and in New York, picking up young men and thoroughly enjoying his life. He returned to Yaddo as assistant to the director for five or six consecutive summers. He was always busy, not only taking care of the guests and working on his paintings, but also going through every closet, every bit of storage space, carefully examining everything he found, and sometimes discovering treasures that were later sold for Yaddo's benefit. He was invited to several other artists' retreats and went to France and New Mexico and worked well. His paintings sold in Boston at the Pucker-Safer Gallery.

David died of AIDS only two months ago, as I write this on July 28, 1993. We, too, had had an affair, but, as David said, it was less out of passion than of affection. We loved each other. He touched me with a tenderness I had never before experienced.

I look at my journal for the period of his last illness and rejoice at the days and nights we had together in the hospital:

11 March, 7:05 A.M. NYUniversity Hospital. David is watching the news on TV as we wait for 7:45 before going up to the 15th floor for breakfast. David has a suite, Room 1189, a bedroom with two beds, bath, TV, telephone, a sitting room with another TV, lounge chairs, refrigerator and a second telephone. Hotel rooms are not often this luxurious. Yesterday we had met with Dr. Greene, middle-aged, bearded, with eyes expressing sympathy and honesty and intelligence. David now has a wasting syndrome, the cause as yet unknown. He lost forty pounds and continues to lose weight. It might be cytomegalovirus or MAI, microbacterial Avian Infection. A Hickman catheter will give him some nourishment. It will be implanted

Walkabout

later today, much like a pacemaker, on the upper chest. There is a complicated list of instructions about sterilization and hooking oneself up to the pump for 12 hours a day (it might be easiest at night), perhaps for the rest of his life.* Doctor Greene wants him to gain 40 pounds. If he does so in the next few months, the catheter might be removed. That is, if the wasting syndrome stops destroying his body. Nothing is definite. If David refuses the Hickman, he will waste away and starve to death. His body does not absorb enough nutrients no matter how much he eats. It all goes through his body without giving back strength. With the Hickman, he will at least have some of the nutriments necessary to life.

My advice last night to David was to have it implanted and to take it from there. Just see what happens in the next weeks. If his body refuses to function properly on its own, he can then make the decision as to whether he wants to continue with the machine, to remove it and waste away, or to do himself in with pills. It is not an easy decision to make. He asked directly what I would do and I told him my truth, that I would first check out the catheter. If it doesn't work I would find the pills and commit suicide. "We are all different," I said. "Particularly me at 71, not to be compared with you at 43."

There is also the problem of where and how he will live when he leaves the hospital. From here, he will go to his sister's house in Queens and she will have to learn to cope with the machine, as well. It is so complicated that a course is given on attaching and detaching the Hickman to the machine. He cannot stay at his sister's forever and doesn't really want to put her and the family out. He wants to go back up to Durham, to his house, and to his dog. He insists that he can get health care up there. Presumably, David's companion, a drug addict, will be with him. He comes to the hospital to stay for several days and nights at a time, rushes back up to Durham to do whatever business he does and always returns much later than he said he would. He is in difficulties himself and finds taking care of David a real burden. He says he will have a breakdown if he continues this way. He broke down last night, saying that he doesn't know how much longer he can cope. David is the most important human being on earth for him but without a break in the routine now and then, he will not be able to get through it. He loves David and would do anything for him, or almost anything, or so he says.

Sometimes, we talk in the dining room when we are alone. He told me his mother used to say to the children, "Go! Go play in the middle of the street., maybe a car will knock you down." His father wasn't much better. He used to take the kids, his own as well as his wife's, in the car and put their fingers into the cigarette lighter and burn them. He is confused and angry. He keeps asking, "Why me?" It doesn't seem to occur to him to ask, "Why David?" He is always ready for his snort of coke or whatever will calm him down. He is sad and I cannot help but feel sorry for him. He starts therapy but doesn't go on with it. Sometimes, I think,

*This turned out to be relatively simple.

62

Walkabout

"Shit man! You are so good-looking, with such a marvelous body. You have so much in your favor. Why are you destroying yourself this way?"

Last night, the nurse said to David, "You look really sick."

Of course, he looks sick, dammit! Down from 155 pounds to 114. Now, with all the other problems, he's anemic. Every day there is something new. We went up to the 14th floor this morning where two vials of blood were taken. We await results. David looks ghastly, like a concentration camp victim, a starving Somali child. He takes his seconal, gets high on it, slurs his speech, falls asleep. He's dehydrated, too, another serious condition. Last night, he spent the hours of 10 P.M. to 1 A.M. on 14 being hydrated. He slept fitfully but is no longer drinking as much liquid as before the re-hydration process. If all goes well the Hickman will be inserted. The companion will be coming back here around 10 this morning, he said, so that I can visit Berenice in St. Vincent's.

Yesterday I called my oldest friend Floriano twice and told him most of what is going on, including the fact that David and I had talked about suicide. David's friend said he could not think about this. "How do you know he won't end up a cripple instead of being dead?" he demanded. He doesn't want to think of a time when David will no longer be alive. He needs to join a drug program. It doesn't do any good to say that it is all his own fault that he's on drugs. That's probably the worst thing I could say to him. He needs a good therapist since he obviously cannot cure himself. He has taken money entrusted to him by David and used it for drugs and has run up a $5,000 phone bill on sex calls to various parts of the world. He drives David mad.

David is asleep now, looking peaceful in spite of his ravaged face. We talked a lot about Allan, formerly a lover of David's, and how he, David, feels guilty for not having paid Allan back the money he borrowed. David has no way of repaying it, but I know Allan, I told him, he would never bug him about money or about anything else, would never stop loving him, never stop helping in every way he can. "He loves you, David!" I told him. "For Christ's sake, he loves you and would never do anything to hurt you in any way. Stop thinking about it. You have enough to worry about without bringing that to mind."

Later, 10 A.M. I hope that companion of David's calls so that I can get to Berenice early this afternoon. St. Vincent's says she is still in the operating room. According to the descriptive material Dr. Liang gave to David, the feeding process is called TPN, Total Parenteral Nutrition. It is a way of providing the body with the nutrition, all the calories it needs by dripping it directly into the blood stream, through the catheter placed in a large vein near the heart. Dr. Liang will put the catheter in after supper tonight.

12 March. Berenice is back home as fit as anyone could be after a laparoscopy. The operation was successful, though it took longer than expected. I saw her and she looks fine. She even showed me the scar; rather, she showed me the tiny bandage over the incision.

Walkabout

Now what about all those fair weather friends of David? Where are they? All are always complaining about being too busy to come to the hospital. Some are even worried that David will die without paying back what he owes them. I talked to Allan late last night. Friends are complaining to him, now, saying right out that they refuse to see David. They are terrified of death and cannot face anyone who is so close to it. How sensible illness and death and mourning are in Asmat. No fear of contact with the sick. No fear of the dead body. Death is part of life, is the normal continuance of life. Without death there can be no new life. They have evolved their own way of adjusting to that kind of change by keeping in touch with the body itself until it has completely decomposed, living with the dead body outside the house on a platform while it disintegrates.

The other day, David and I talked of our own limited sexual relationship. He said something I cannot forget. "It is not that we had sex together, we had love." It was an expression of purity and great affection. Had we continued the sexual relationship we might have fallen out as friends and I am grateful for whatever we had together. Now, at death's door we could talk about it, as I'm sure he has done with Allan. Their friendship and love is permanent, perhaps with a bit of volatile expressiveness at times. But the way David lights up when Allan walks into the hospital room is enough to make one feel the power of their love and the beauty of their friendship. We have discovered new facets of one another. By being with David twenty-four hours a day, learning to give and to receive, learning to clean him up, to lift him out of the bathtub or put him into it, talking, listening, sharing, not only with David but with Allan at the same time or separately, alone, telling one another of our secret secrets, we all opened up to one another, left nothing unsaid.

13 March, at home. Had dinner this evening with my dear friend Dorle Soria. I took her home in a cab yesterday afternoon. David's friend says that the TPN is giving David urinary problems. The nurse buzzed the room at 5:30 this morning to have the friend take David back from Observation to his own room. Allan called to say he is coming up from North Carolina for a week or so to stay with David.

17 March, back in hospital. What a difference in David! It is surely miraculous. Suddenly, yesterday, the TPN kicked in. Still no word on what is causing the wasting syndrome, but David is much stronger or appears to be so. Allan came early yesterday and Jeannette another painter friend, came for a while. Lillian, David's sister, and her son Albert came. She too has been spending nights here. It is a remarkable way of treating patients, with visitors about to spend 24 hours with the patient. Rosemary Beck, an old teacher of David's, came and others came, Laine, Melissa, Hilma and Morty, all friends who had met David at Yaddo, just as I did. Allan is simply here, not wanting to work, not able to work, not until after he has had a good amount of time with David. Allan is so loving and generous, aware, intelligent, articulate. Needless to say, David is in heaven with him around. Oh,

Walkabout

David! David! How beautiful you are, ravages of body and all. Your spirit, the look from those soulful eyes of yours. I love you. *We* love you! Something in us wells up and reaches out to you, helplessly trying to give you some kind of peace. It stretches in a direct line, heart to heart, mind to mind, eye to eye. We gossip like mad, the three of us, about Yaddo, about all our mutual friends—who is winning prizes, whose book is being made into a film, who is having an opening at Holly Solomon's, what publisher accepted whose book, what movies are around, what plays, music, readings. Yak, yak, yak. It was great, no serious talk, just fun and laughter. Certainly then, no talk of death, only later. Allan is affectionate and loving. He is one of the most whole people I've ever known, one of the dearest on earth. He has a true sense of balance about life and work, and about love. He always astonishes me. Lillian said she would stay until 11 this evening so I accepted Allan's invitation to a book party for Catherine Shine's "Rameau's Niece." The party was at Barocco's restaurant on Church and Franklin. Melissa, Hilma and Morty were also there. Then, Allan and I went to the 211 for dinner. He dropped me at the hospital at 9 o'clock. Lillian went home. Allan will be back tomorrow morning to spend several days. It is one of the wonders of this method of treating patients, that relatives and friends must stay the entire time, usually 24 hours at a stretch. We talked about David and the wonderful times we've had together. Later, we reminisced again with David about our lives and loves and the love we have for one another. It brought us still closer.

18 March. Perhaps my last morning at the hospital, depending upon David's progress. He came in at 114 pounds, is now up to 118. He still has no appetite for food and eats nothing. David's sister Lillian too wants to give more time here, though it is possible that David will be leaving for Lillian's house in Queens this weekend. The TPN is still attached to David at 6:30 A.M. There are several AIDS patients here, skeletons of men, of women.

25 March, my birthday. David is at his sister's in Queens and is remarkably better. He came by my apartment yesterday and we had lunch together with his nephews, handsome creatures. Amazing how David seems to have come back to life. Dinner tonight at Floriano's.

6 April. Ramon is finally in hospital where he should have been from the moment he returned to New York from his trip to the Philippines. He has pneumocystis cariini pneumonia, aside from the Kaposi's sarcoma on his leg and heaven alone knows what else, I wondered what was going on and why Dr. Bellman had not put him in the hospital before this but Ramon is in such an odd mood that he leaves me bewildered about the truth of his condition. He is in denial about his AIDS, which is normal, of course. He refuses to acknowledge how ill he is, also normal and understandable. It must be that the cytomegalovirus has begun to affect his brain, or maybe it is the drugs he is taking. I realize that this lying, arrogant, aggressive, selfish person is not the Ramon who has been such an important part of my life, not the Ramon I knew and with whom I fell in love, the Ramon I still love deeply. There is no way that I can allow anything to interfere with the love I have had for him.

Ramon and I met through Elliott Stein as we were leaving Alice Tully Hall, after a film preview. We had lunch together or perhaps it was tea in the afternoon. He made my heart beat faster. Intelligent, handsome, Filipino, I pursued him. He didn't object.

Both Ramon and David have been in denial about their AIDS and their future, both of them testing themselves to the very limit of endurance, David running around from one auction to another before his previous hospital stay, and buying useless items, using money that is not available, both of them on the go all the time, Ramon in particular rushing from movie house to theater to looking at videos, not sitting still for a moment to assess life and illness, borrowing money every other day, wanting to take in everything that is out there, oh, it is Ramon, all right. He hasn't lost the weight that David lost but the change is striking in the way he looks, in the look in his eyes "of fear" almost alternating with blankness, the gray color of his skin, the loss of muscle tone, the inability to focus eyes and mind, and of course the molluscum on his face, a skin condition characterized by ugly tumors. I talked with Dr. Bellman who said that the psychological symptoms I described were commonplace with CMV patients and that he had been aware of Ramon's dementia for some time. Still, the effect of the drugs he was taking then cannot be ruled out as contributing to his condition. Until this stay in St. Vincent's, Ramon had refused AZT. But now he has agreed to it, as well as to other drugs. Damn! What a shitty time for me to be leaving for Fiji and the ship! I was then lecturing on a cruise ship that sailed from Indonesia to the South Pacific, for years, the only way I had of earning money.

I arrived in Fiji on April 17, leaving David and Ramon behind. I was doing my job, talking about the cultures and arts of the people we were visiting. When I had left New York, David was well enough to be going to antique fairs with Paul. Ramon was deteriorating in St. Vincent's, being visited by friends and by his mother, who had come from the Philippines. His sisters also came, one from Florida, and the other from Massachusetts. I would hear nothing of either David or Ramon until my return, partly because I had asked Allan and others not to send bad news—I could hear it all when I got back—and partly because of the uncertainty of mail delivery in the ports to which I was headed on the ship, the *Spice Islander*. We rarely went to islands that had post offices. The final entry in my journal is dated June 13, 1993, Saigon, and takes up the last pages of the book. I had heard nothing and returned expecting the worst. I called Lillian and got the machine, and then called Allan: "Oh, Toby, the news is bad. David died. The funeral took place ten days ago." We talked for some time.

I called Ramon's number, and he answered, "I'm fine. I'm off to Texas next week to work on a video for Amnesty International. Then, I'm going to Arizona and New Mexico and to San Diego and to San Francisco." Astonishingly, there was Ramon looking healthy and happy, back to his old, loving, affectionate self! What a beautiful human being!

Allan worked on his novel in Chapel Hill and, late in June, went up to Yaddo to read at the benefit and to write. He had asked for a three-week stay. We were hoping that our time here would overlap so we could talk at length about David and resolve our feelings, but we were to miss each other by one day. When Allan discovered this bad luck, he called and said, "Toby, come up one day early, and I will stay an extra day. I'll take a room for us at the Adelphi so we can spend the night together." And we did, finally saying all we wanted to say. In a letter that just arrived, Allan writes, "David's more clearly and fondly on my mind these days—Brahmsian melancholy over his helpless eternal elegance—he never lost it, God be praised—for that, at least."

Hanging up on Allan was difficult. I wanted the connection between us to go on and on. Releasing him, breaking the connection, meant realizing the death of David, making it all too present. I sat in my rocking chair with my plants around me, alive and well, with the Hudson below me, the sea bass still laying their eggs on the rotting pilings of the pier. A study of landfill at that Bank Street pier meant the death of all the fish there. The tide was going out, the sea bass that saved us from housing in front of my windows, running with the current, the clouds over New Jersey being swept northward by gentle winds, billowing, everything I could see and feel in movement, everything living, growing, but David dead, gone.

In Asmat, I would have wailed, let out great cries of anguish as soon as I learned of David's death. I would have stripped naked, rolled around in the mud, expressed aloud in front of everyone my deepest feelings, let it all out.

In Asmat, the concept of life and death is different from that of the West; at least, it was when I first arrived there in 1973. Head-hunting continued in the remoter regions then, and may still be practiced in parts of the foothills of the Jayawijaya Mountains. That area, however, is beyond the boundaries of Asmat territory. Warfare, cannibalism, and surprise attacks were still everyday events in the 1950s in Asmat proper, so everyone understood the closeness of death. The people had evolved a culture of revenge that kept them in constant contact with the spirit world; they had developed a mythology that explained and excused violence against others. All deaths were attributed to magic performed by enemies; therefore, the spirits of those recently killed demanded vengeance before they would set off for Safan, Land of the Dead.

My oldest friend among the Asmat was David Simni. I had met him early in my first stay there and had taken an instant liking to this affable elderly man in spite of his asking for tobacco every time we met. I later learned that his family was always sending him to me for tobacco and taking most of it when he returned to Sjuru. He was the oldest man in his village and may have been the oldest in all of Asmat. He had only four or five teeth left, so his chin folded up toward his nose, leaving little space between them. Even so, he had a smile that seemed to encompass his whole face and formed a series of wrinkles around the slits of his eyes. He wore his hair short, mostly a pepper-and-salt stubble that spread from head to unshaven face. He was so thin that the hollows of his cheeks were like black holes. His whole body, bent, was more knobs than flesh, the skin hanging loosely. Once or twice a week he came to the museum to ask me for tobacco. He carried a long stick to help keep himself upright. He wore ragged shorts and was bare-chested and bare-footed most of the time. He was respected because of his age, which may have been sixty or sixty-five, although he looked to be in his nineties. Still, he was not considered important as a headman and was never asked his opinion on village matters. He was sad and old. He had never taken a head in battle, the prime requisite for leadership, a war chief or a chief of feasts. He was a gentle man, not in the least violent in the manner of my adoptive father Ndocemen. The tender expression on Simni's face was in stunning contrast to the ferocity and force to be seen on Ndocemen's. His name, in fact, translates as "I, penis." He was the first in Asmat to adopt me.

The first time Simni came to the museum, he did not enter, but, in traditional fashion, stood outside the door and coughed to make his presence known. He coughed so softly that I did not hear him. After several minutes, he coughed louder. I went to the door and invited him in. He opened his mouth in awe, looked around with his eyes, but did not move his head, and then looked down. I gestured for him to sit on the floor and sat there with him. He whispered into my ear, even though no one else was around.

"Tombias," he said. "Tombias, *Minta, tambaku.*" I got up and went to the cabinet in which I kept the spiced tobacco so beloved by the Asmat, broke a piece from the plug, and handed it to Simni. He took off the magic bag he wore hanging from his neck. It was made of interwoven sago leaf and was decorated with the white feathers of the sulphur-crested cockatoo. He removed everything from the bag: a small knife given to him by Brother Mark, one of the missionaries there; some small bones and teeth that might have come from rats; some larger bones and a small animal skull; pieces of nipa leaf for rolling cigarettes; and a small pipe, also given to him by Brother Mark. He loosened the tobacco and stuffed it into his pipe. "*Api?*" he asked. I brought him fire and a box of matches, and he lit his pipe. He smoked contentedly for a while.

Walkabout

We did not speak. He puffed, relit the pipe, puffed. The memories, the thoughts that might have gone through him filled me with a passion for the Asmat that lasted for days, during my time awake and my time asleep. In some ways we were a pair, for he was a peaceful man, never wanting to kill, never wanting to go on raids. Perhaps he was unique, perhaps not. Perhaps most Asmat never wanted to go into battle. They are happier now, they say, now that there is no longer any head-hunting, now that warfare, for the most part, is gone. They can go about their daily lives without fear of attack, can go in their canoes past other villages and paddle to Agats to buy canned sardines and tobacco when there is money.

After some minutes, David Simni stood up and looked around the display room. He went directly to an exhibit of *Syrinx aruanus* shells, picked up the largest one, about thirteen inches long, and placed it against his abdomen at the navel, in the position at which he would have worn it had he been a great headhunter. He held it in one hand, patting and stroking it with the other. He nestled it at his shoulder, cradled it in the crook of his elbow. He moaned and exclaimed, "Aduh!" as he ran his hand over the trumpet-like shell. Tears appeared at his cheeks. He seemed to be reliving a piece of his past, perhaps regretting lost opportunities, perhaps satisfied they never had happened. He replaced the shell and slowly began walking around the room, dragging his feet on the ironwood floor. "Aduh!" he whispered again. He touched the base of one of the great ancestor poles. He moved to other displays, picked up traditional artifacts, and ignored those that had been made for sale. He had an unerring instinct for what was real and had been made for use in daily life—such as paddles, drums, spears, and bamboo horns—and what had been carved for specific rituals and feasts—such as ancestor poles, shields, prowheads, and body masks. Even artifacts that were outside his area of knowledge were easily understood by his eye, just as David Vereano had instantly understood the difference between real and fake antiques. David Simni was my litmus paper, my expert in recognizing traditional works as opposed to those made specifically for sale. David Vereano, as young as he was, as unschooled as he was, had the knack of being part of the culture from which an artifact came, so he knew its history without having seen the object before. David Simni, as old as he was, still had the same knack, although necessarily in a much narrower world.

Sjuru, the village in which David Simni lived, was about a mile's walk over a dangerously dilapidated walkway from Agats, capital of the District of Asmat. Agats was where the Indonesian government had its headquarters, where the police and army were stationed, and, more recently, where a post office had been built and an office of the Coast Guard opened. Agats is also the home base of the Crosier missionaries. The bishop is the owner of the museum. Often, from my house, close to the convent, I could hear people wailing in Sjuru, a sound that was quite distinct, that drifted over the swamp to all of Agats. It signaled that a death had occurred or would happen any time soon.

At one o'clock in the morning of November 10, 1978, the wailing woke me. It wasn't difficult to assume that Simni had died. I went back to sleep and got up at 5:30, had a peanut butter sandwich, and walked to Sjuru, arriving at Simni's house just after sunrise. The house was crowded with people of the village, some of whom made way for me. There were no greetings, just as in Jewish families there are no greetings under the same circumstances. The wailing had changed from shrillness to a moaning sound. Simni's body, in the darkness of early morning, was hardly discernible in the mass of people. The blanket I had given him three weeks earlier covered his body, but not his face. His sunken cheeks were deep in shadow, the bones highlighted by the light coming in through the doorway. His closed eyes, too, were sunken. There was a deep sadness to his features, as though he, too, were mourning. On top of the blanket were fifteen *Syrinx aruanus* shells, a number of bride-price stone axes, and one metal ax, all indicating the great man he was at that moment of death. Perhaps he had been violent in his youth; if so, he had never revealed that side of himself to me. I quickly rejected the thought: he was a gentle man.

Ndocemen, my adoptive father, led me to a place of honor at Simni's head, which rested on one of the knees of his red-haired widow, Marta Ausekom. She was giving the dead body of Simni what consolation she could give, her delicate fingers running over his face. The plaintive wailing turned into a piercing sound. Marta cried out Simni's name over and over. There were no tears. Ndocemen straddled Simni's body. He sang of Simni's exploits, calling out the names of enemies he might or might not have killed, giving him a false early life, full of the violence he so abhorred. Perhaps he himself wanted to become part of the mythology of Sjuru as a great headhunter. Remembering the fragility of Simni's body when I last saw him, it was difficult to imagine him as a taker of heads or imagine his life as a series of fierce encounters.

The house was more or less divided into two big rooms. In typical Asmat fashion, there was no furniture. Everyone ate and slept on the bamboo floor, close to the fire. Except for the women at Simni's head and feet, those surrounding him were men, sitting densely packed together. Every once in a while, women got up and danced, not the usual Asmat movement of knocking the knees together in imitation of a cassowary, but stepping first on one foot several times, and then on the other. One of the women seemed entranced, dancing with her arms straight out, her hands first flapping and then going up and together as though in blessing. Older women danced more vigorously than the young, with movements resembling the pounding of the pith of a sago tree and the paddling of a canoe. They might have been making the food for Simni to take along as he paddled his way to the Land of the Dead. Digging sticks and paddles were brought in and became part of the dance.

Two women straddled the body and danced above Simni. They threw themselves onto the floor, stripped off their only garment, the *awer,* ran out of the house, and rolled in the mud, the only time a woman may appear naked in public. Rolling in the mud covered body smells, making it impossible for Simni's spirit to recognize them and enter their bodies, like a dybbuk.

Marta Ausekom transferred Simni's head into my lap. I looked down and stroked his cheek. I wailed with the others. Marta got up, still wailing, went out of the house, and stripped off her *awer* at the edge of the river. All the women in the house took up their paddles, digging sticks, and bows and arrows, went outside, and danced through the whole village.

Ndocemen straddled Simni's body once again and danced. He bent at the knees, raising his arms and slapping them down onto his thighs, with a loud clap. Suddenly he was a bird, perhaps a mythical creature. When he stopped and went off, Siretsj, one of the great elders of Sjuru, threw himself down onto the body and wailed. He was naked, his testicles bloated from filariasis.

The wailing came in waves, sometimes everyone wailing loudly, sometimes only a few mourners wailing softly. Men took me to the fireplace and fed me sago and shrimp. A carpenter came in and measured Simni's body length with a ruler. He was putting the coffin together outside the house. It had become the law in Asmat that the dead were to be buried in the village cemetery and not left to rot close to the family house in the village. The smell of the decomposing body was overpowering. Burial of the body in the mud was not traditional.

Women massaged the necks of their men, pressing a hand to the forehead, the other hand to the nape of the neck. They pressed and squeezed the flesh of the shoulders and back. Everyone's body ached from sitting; everyone was dripping with perspiration.

When the coffin was ready, Simni's body was carried out of the house and placed in the coffin. Women took the shells and stone axes back to their houses. A machete was put next to the body. A sarong and the blanket went in as well. The coffin was carried to the men's house, where it was surrounded by all the men of Sjuru. Ndocemen sang of other exploits of Simni, and the coffin was nailed shut. Only a few people followed it to the village cemetery. Mourning for most of Sjuru was over. Simni was one of the earliest Asmat whose body was placed whole into a coffin and buried in the mud of the cemetery.

The members of Simni's family shaved their heads. Marta Ausekom put on her mourning garments: a hat that folded around her head, making it difficult to see her face; a breast band; a hip band; armbands; leg bands; tassels that hung from her neck; and tassels that went down her back. All were made of sago leaf or fiber. She was bent over, her eyes staring only at the ground.

Marta Ausekom wailed periodically for several days, going fishing in the morning with one of her sisters, pounding sago when necessary, doing all the normal household duties. At night, she wailed. The spectacle, the rituals, had cleaned the body and spirit of Simni and had cleansed the village. He was on his way to Safan. His spirit would not stay around Sjuru and give problems to his family, as it would have done in other times, when it would have sought vengeance. My gentle friend went on into the darkness of the spirit world.

6

Change

In a book called *Letters to a Young Doctor*, Richard Selzer writes of disposable knives and syringes:

We are too removed from our tools. It is a kind of betrayal of our craft. Because we do not make our instruments with our own hands, we do not use them to best advantage. Our relationship to our instruments is a more distant and formal one than were it still necessary to chisel the knob of a knife from a stone or sharpen a goose quill to a probe. A great oboist cuts and ties his own reeds. So does the fisherman his trout flies. In so doing these men infuse them with their spirit. If the gift of prophecy has not deserted me, I should say that such men will make sweeter music and catch bigger fish than those who place the craft in the hands of manufacturers. There is something soulless about a steel blade that is punched out identical to all others by a machine, is used one time and then discarded.*

Asmat carvers use their tools almost daily. Before long, new tools are worn to a shiny patina of black, as are the metal chisels made from nails with wooden handles that some carvers have been using for the better part of this century. The hafts have been molded by use into the shape of the owner's hand, much like old work gloves, caked and cracked with mud, take on the shape and humanness of the palms that wear them. Carvers who live close to the mouth of the huge Betsj River have long since discarded the old bone and stone tools in favor of the metal ones they them-

*Richard Selzer, *Letters to a Young Doctor* (New York: Simon and Schuster, 1982), 114.

selves made from nails found in wooden planks floating upstream with the tide. The nails were pounded at one end with stone on metal on stone until the desired shape was reached, with a width of not much more than a quarter of an inch. It was the only metal they had ever seen.

Carvers made astonishing artifacts with this narrow tool, including ancestor poles as high as thirty feet, although the carvings were roughed out with stone axes, and then with steel when it became available.

You never know how influences on people begin, whether it is as subtle as the changes that come through the use of metal tools or as simple as the changes brought on by the wearing of clothing. Clothing, in fact, was a subject that the bishop brought up at our first meeting at the museum in Agats: "Never take extra clothing along with you when you go on a collecting trip. It is the worst spreader of skin disease, and the Asmat do not need that. They have enough problems."

Early on, in the 1950s, a few carvers tried the machine-made chisels given to them by missionaries or later by tourists who brought them in, eager to use them as trade items. These tools, however, were found wanting at first and were quickly rejected. The flat steel edge had no give, no warmth, no quality of life that passed into the carver's own hands and body. Today chisels and nails are for sale in some of the trade stores, and the young carvers have taken to them, to the detriment of the carvings they work on, for these men have not yet learned or felt that spirit pass into them. Nails in planks are no longer to be found, for few wooden ships now sail past the region of Asmat, except for the relatively small fishing boats brought in from Sulawesi.

I learned about the nails from Fabianus Owat, an elderly carver who, as a youth, had known enough of the Indonesian language to become the first translator for Father Gerard Zegwaard, the first missionary to settle in Asmat, in 1953. I was prompted to search out the origins of metal, from where and when it had come to Asmat, after I had seen a war shield in the Rijksmuseum voor Volkerkunde in Leiden, Holland, that obviously had been carved with metal tools. It had been given to the museum and was cataloged in 1906 by a member of the first Dutch military expedition to enter the area. This was long before it was learned that stone, which does not exist in the swamps of Asmat, had been traded down from the foothills of the Jayawijaya Mountains. Westerners did not yet know that people lived there.

Indeed, nothing was known of the existence of the peoples of the Grand Balim Valley, in the midst of the snow-covered mountains, until Richard Archbold flew over the valley in 1938 and decided that the patterns on the ground were so formal that they had to have been made by human hands. He led an expedition there under the aegis of the American

Museum of Natural History and discovered the Dani and Jali peoples. The patterns on the ground turned out to be their gardens of yams.

Asmat, too, was unknown at that time, except by the few traders who traveled the rivers in search of crocodile skins. The Asmat were known to be violent headhunters who practiced cannibalism. They were first contacted in 1770 by two boatloads of men from Captain James Cook's *Endeavour*. The British sailors landed in what was later named Cook Bay, on the South Casuarina coast of Asmat, but they immediately retreated in the face of what they thought of as an attack.

I had been asking about the origins of metal in dozens of villages without learning anything when the answer came from Fabianus Owat in Atsj, a large village with a population of about 2,000. It is on the Betsj River, close to where it flows into the shallow Arafura Sea, so shallow, in fact, that navigators who do not know the area well often run aground and must await the next high tide, hoping for the ship to float off. Kedging, or pulling a ship along by hauling on the cable of an anchor carried out from the ship and dropped, is not possible in Asmat, where there is little difference between the water and the mud beneath it. There is nothing solid for the kedge to grab hold of in order to pull itself off a bar of mud.

"Oh, yes," said Fabianus. "We have had these tools for a very long time, since before the white man came to Asmat. Old planks of wood with nails in them from wrecked ships sometimes floated up the Betsj from the sea when the water was coming in. We pulled out the nails and pounded them into chisels with stones. We even had a special name for them, *kas ndes.*"

Fabianus was rarely seen walking around Atsj or sitting on his family porch without his cuscus-fur headband. An inner section of a chambered nautilus shell dangled from it onto his forehead. He normally inserted into the headband two sticks onto which the white feathers of the sulphur-crested cockatoo were glued. A cuscus is a vicious marsupial about the size of a cat; its fur is worn by all Asmat, including children. Fabianus wore a nosepiece only on special occasions. His nose was huge, as are those of all older Asmat who have been wearing nosepieces all their lives, stretching a tiny hole first pierced in the septum just before initiation rites, when the boys and girls might be seven or eight years old. The hole through Fabianus's septum was large enough for me to see through to the other side even when I sat a few feet away. I do not remember that he ever wore earlobe decorations, although there were holes in his lobes.

Fabianus was a specialist in carving decorated paddles. He liked to incise the blade with a design called *fatsjep,* the curled tail of a cuscus. He also carved the heads of hornbills at the top end of the pole of the paddle.

"Are those designs you are working on called *jirmbi?*" I asked with feigned innocence, hoping to impress Fabianus with design information I had learned in Amanamkai, a village around the bend of the As River, the River of Shit. *Jirmbi* is the head of a hornbill. He laughed and shook his head. "If you look closely," he said, pointing to the beak of one of the finished heads, "you will see that there are no cuts in the birds' beaks. That means that I am working on *tsjenepir,* pelican heads. If you look up into the evening sky, you will see them flying up the As River. They are only here for a short time, and then fly away. I carve them only while they are here in the Atsj area." I had already heard about the periodical migrations of pelicans from Australia. This was the first time I had heard of and saw the design of the pelican and would now be able to recognize instantly the difference between *tsjenepir* and *jirmbi.* I had also heard that in English, the *jirmbi,* the hornbill, is also known as the yearbird because the notches in the bird's beak tell the age of the bird: five notches for a five-year-old, three notches for a three-year-old.

Fabianus and I would sit and talk until dusk. By that time, the women would be returning from their fishing expeditions. They would bank their canoes in the mud at low tide or, at high tide, would tie their lines to poles sticking up from knee-deep water. They would be coming home with food in time to make the evening meal. They walked in front of us, carrying their two-woman fishing nets, their bags of catfish, and their long tubes of slightly brackish drinking water from the darkest pools in the forest.

Father Virgil Petermeier, another of the Crosiers, was pastor of Atsj early in my stay in Asmat. He put me up for weeks and took me around the village, sat with me in the men's house, and translated. We had arrived in Asmat for the first time within a few months of each other, but he was further ahead in his understanding of the Indonesian language. We both knew, however, that Asmat was a much more difficult language to learn. He took me on patrol around his parish and introduced me to a young couple in Sogoni who were Protestant missionaries and who seemed delightful and intelligent until I mentioned that I was collecting artifacts for the museum.

"Products of Satan!" they said simultaneously. "You won't find any carvings here. We burned them all. We even burned their drums so they could not sing their songs to provoke one another into warfare. We broke up their war shields, too." It was a pronouncement that seemed to encompass both Virgil and me, as though we agreed that the destruction of the artifacts was necessary. They were obviously very proud of themselves. The carvings were often hidden away. I went around the village to see what I could find. Virgil, always the essence of politeness, stayed with the attractive-looking couple until my return. After all, we had just been served a fine lunch of canned foods and fresh fruit that had been flown in from the United States.

Change

Since Virgil appeared to be so friendly with the young couple, the villagers were afraid to let him know that they still had a few of the old artifacts. They did not want the rest of their carvings to be confiscated. Later in the day, when we had left Sogoni far behind, I broached the subject with Virgil. "I do not like to say anything about the artifacts," he said. "It is a subject on which I disagree with them. But that is their business."

I did talk to some of the people. "Oh, no!" they said, at first. "We have nothing left. Everything was burned. We are allowed to sing only their songs. No more feasts." After an hour or so, one of the villagers relented and brought out a head-hunting horn of bamboo. It was beautifully incised with designs of a wiggling snake, *asuk fofasi*. "May I trade with some knives for this?" I asked.

They were very enthusiastic. "Oh, yes! Oh, yes!" they said. "We have many other pieces in our homes." But they would not show them to me. In fact, I left without the horn. The people had backed out of our arrangement at the last minute. It impressed me deeply that they wanted to keep as many of their carvings as possible. I never found out what they had hidden away—if, indeed, they did have hidden objects.

The Asmat have a particular sensitivity in their relationship with their personal property. I had just traded for a pig-bone nosepiece, an *otsj*, carved in the design of a banyan-tree root. It was about five inches long and perhaps half an inch in diameter. The bone was held out to me, obviously an offering by a man who might have been thirty years old. The man was obviously enthralled with the goods with which I wanted to trade, especially the knives. We quickly made the deal, and he went off with a smile on his face. Two hours later, the man was back, crying uncontrollably. He told me that he wanted the *otsj* back, that it was named for his father and he could not let it go. I handed the piece back to him and let him keep the knife.

Nail tools are still in use, as well as some traditional tools, including mussel shells that the Asmat use as scrapers, the only implement that satisfies their craving for the smooth surface needed on certain artifacts, such as paddles, spears, arrows, digging sticks, and drums. Nothing manufactured can offer the smoothness and sheen of this sharp-edged shell, which fits so easily into the palm of the hand.

Another traditional tool necessary to the performance of various rituals is the bamboo knife, which has an edge at least as sharp as that of steel, although it quickly becomes blunt. In the past, the Asmat used bamboo knives to decapitate enemy heads and cut up the rest of the body. The strict regulations that governed this ritual demanded the use of a bamboo knife in the cutting process. Pigs were slaughtered and butchered in the same way, and still are in certain villages. The Asmat also continue to use pig-bone awls and drills to make holes in shells and seeds, to crochet men's hair, and to crochet fiber string into parts of body masks. They also use human bone for the points of harpoons.

Tools sometimes dictate the kind of carving to be done and the extent to which it is refined. The delicate ajour* of the villages of Amanamkai and Atsj could not have been executed with stone and bone; the body of the carving is too thin, too fragile for the use of such tools. Although comparatively rough during the first year of experiments with the new concept, the quality changed so drastically that I was surprised and pleased with the new works. The smoothness was exceptional. It delighted me that all the symbols remained traditional: star stone axes, carved human figures, carved decapitated heads, the curled tail of a cuscus.

I talked to Father H. von Peij when he came on a short return visit to Asmat in the 1970s. He had lived in Asmat for two years when Irian was still under Dutch control, twenty years earlier. "In a sense," he said, "ajour are the artistic descendants of the prowheads of war canoes. I introduced the idea of the ajour and gave them that name.

"I took a plank from the lumber mill and cut it to the size of an ordinary canoe prowhead. On the panel I drew three human figures in profile. I asked Nikolaus Kow to cut out the spaces between the lines, as if the panel were a prowhead. The figures were seated, with elbows on knees, the 'praying mantis' design. There was a series of intricately carved ancestor figures with the head-hunting symbols of the black palm cockatoo and the spiral shell nosepiece motif that represents the tusks of a wild boar."

The first finished pieces came out coarsely carved. Although unrefined in every sense, they had the feel of interesting work. The Asmat ordinarily know when to stop carving, but these works were under outside influence. All the important pieces they produced in the twentieth century had no smoothness or polish; they were, in fact, crude to a Westerner's eye. The crudely hewn quality is partly what gave the carvings their power. Although the roughness continued during the first months of experiments, the carvings slowly became more and more polished. The character of the carvings over time changed to the extent that I was deeply delighted at first when I later saw some of them in the recreation room of the Catholic mission. The carvings sometimes depicted human spirits and sometimes spirits of the forest. Sometimes they were completely abstract; sometimes, realistic.

I was particularly delighted with the beauty of the sheen, the elegance, the meticulousness with which the artifacts were made. However, I felt

*The word is from the French, meaning "pierced," and describes a certain openwork carving of the Asmat.

that something was lost when delicacy took precedence over the purpose of the carving, that the artistic value declined with the scrupulousness and grace in the manner of carving. It reminded me of the Taj Mahal when I first saw it from the entrance gate, a masterpiece of design and architecture, a great work of art, I thought to myself. Or so I felt when I looked at the reflecting pool and noted the outer atmosphere of the tomb from the distance—until I went up close and went inside. Until I saw those overly worked walls, the filigreed decoration everywhere. It was beautiful, no question of that, but, again, something was lost in all that overloaded lacework. After talking to Father von Peij, it struck me that he was interested in the carvings, but did not see the difference between art and decoration.

Other carvers took to the idea of the ajour because von Peij immediately paid hard cash for the work, and the carvers saw an opportunity for earning money, a rarity in Asmat at that time. Succeeding carvers continued to refine their works, making them more and more delicate, finally smoothing them to a burnished quality with shell. This was possible because the ajour were then being made of ironwood. It wasn't long before the ajour became one of the most desirable, if also the most easily broken, of all the artifacts made in Asmat. Styles in art, of course, are subject to change, and the ajour disappeared after a few years, when it became obvious that the refinement that made them so delicate, also made them vulnerable to breakage.

Von Peij, a short, aggressive man, delighted in discussions about the carvings. We rarely agreed about what was good and what was not. To him, the more polished a work, the more it attracted his eye and purse. He may also have been partly responsible for a type of carving that intrigued and confused me for years, a group of works that I liked immensely. Even though based on traditional designs, they were completely original. They were made of ironwood, about five feet tall, a series of vertically connected carved lozenge shapes, wonderfully thought out. They reminded me of the work of Isamu Noguchi, although the pieces were immediately recognizable as Asmat. They obviously had been conceived as the roots of a banyan tree, which is sacred to the Asmat and an important symbol in their art. Some of the sculptures had a human head carved at the top; others had the head at the bottom; some had both.

Father Johnny Fleischhacker insisted that he had found several of the carvings in one of the warehouses in his parish in Jamasj: "They must have been collected by Smitty before his death, when he was pastor here. I'll bet they were carved by that old war chief Bare. Dammit! He knew a lot about carving and must have been a great warrior." Fleischhacker was always pleased when he had a chance to use an expletive. The attribution to Bare was never confirmed, even though I took photos of the carvings to the men's house in Jamasj and asked everyone about their derivation. No one recognized them. I had never been convinced of their origins in Jamasj, anyway. The style, although modern, pertained more to the traditions of the south of Asmat than to the northwest, where Jamasj was located.

Father von Peij himself told me much later that he had gone to the coastal village of Per to ask the chief, Kokoputsj, an excellent carver with whom he got along well, to produce a crucifix. Kokoputsj was already familiar with carvings and photos of paintings and sculptures of Christ on the Cross, made in the West. Von Peij had related the story of Christ on the Cross, with particular attention given to the end of his life, when he reappeared three days after the Crucifixion. Kokoputsj translated this story into Asmat thought and carved these remarkable lozenge-shaped pieces.

"Banyan trees are sacred to the Asmat," von Peij quoted him as saying. "We place the bodies of women who have died in childbirth in their roots, because it is there that the great spirits live."

Father Smit, according to von Peij, had had no connection with the carvers of those pieces. However, he had spent more time in Agats than he had in his own village of Jamasj and therefore had plenty of opportunities to meet and talk to Kokoputsj. He could easily have bought the carvings directly from him. The village of Per, where Kokoputsj lived, is only a few hours away by paddled canoe.

The Asmat are often confused by the line between ownership and workmanship. A man who commissions a shield to be made often identifies so closely with the spirit within it, a spirit of a relative he himself has named, that with time he assumes the role of the carver as well as that of the commissioner. He takes on that impersonation, completely unaware that he is doing so. But this can work in other ways, as well.

I remember a day in Agats, when Leo Bini came into the museum with a group of other men from Jamasj. All were carrying pandanus mats in which carvings had been wrapped. Leo was a relatively tall man, perhaps five feet ten inches, with scars on his face that might have come from battle with another warrior or from some disease unknown to me. His face was also pitted as though from smallpox, but smallpox did not exist there or anywhere else in New Guinea at that time. He had the kind of build that Westerners admire in men who exercise regularly. He had an outstandingly muscular chest and abdomen developed through standing in the canoe and paddling almost every day of his youth and adult life.

The men took out the carvings. We sat on the ironwood floor while they slowly broke up the plug of spiced tobacco I had put down, wrapped the tobacco in nipa leaves, and smoked contentedly. We negotiated. Two war shields were the most interesting of the works they had brought with them, but, as often as not, when carvers came from distant villages to sell their works, I bought them all to encourage them to continue carving.

"But look here, Leo," I said. "Look at this." I held up one of the non-traditional plaques that were popular with Westerners for a while. It was another kind of panel, made of ironwood and about fifteen by thirty inches. It was heavy. The entire surface was in relief as though it were a shield. "Look at this, Leo. It is very well carved, but it is not *asli;* it is not traditional. It is beautifully worked, but it is not truly Asmat."

"Yes! Yes, it is," Leo said. "Just look here, Tombias." He pointed to a group of several incised spirals. His index finger traced one of them. "Look at this *fatsjep,* the curled tail of a cuscus. We have always carved this motif. And here is the *was wow,* the clearing in the jungle. Here is the *asuk jak,* the intestines of worms. Here is *asuk fofasi,* wiggling snake, and here is *tarep,* flying fox feet. Tombias, it is *asli.*"

"But Leo, " I countered, "this plaque is nothing like the works you have carved before. It looks more like the surface of a shield."

"Yes it is *asli,* yes it is." Leo was disconcerted. "It is a shield, too, a *djemesj.* Just look more carefully. It is a shield, only it is smaller. It is for children to use in learning about warfare. It is like the small bows and arrows we make for the children with which to practice shooting." He was trying hard to convince me that the plaque was traditional in concept. The other men nodded and grunted with every statement he made, agreeing with it all, whether they thought it was true or not. They wanted to be sure of payment.

"Leo, look at the back; it doesn't even have a handle. And you never had shields made of ironwood. Too difficult to carve and too heavy to carry."

"No, but before we had metal tools, it was almost impossible to carve ironwood with stone or bone, or bamboo or shell. That is why we used softer wood."

"Tell me, Leo," I said, showing him a shield about six feet tall. "What about this particular shield. Can you tell me who the carver is and where the shield came from?" A couple of hours earlier, when the men from Jamasj had arrived in Agats, I saw Leo Bini among them. I went into the storage room and took out a shield whose provenance was on a label hanging from its handle. The label read, "Carver: Leo Bini, Jamasj Village, 1971." It had been collected twenty years earlier. I removed the label.

"Here, Leo, I want you to tell me who carved this particular shield." I looked at it carefully. It was beautiful. The entire outer shape of the shield was that of a penis, with, at the top, the head of a rayfish, but with eyes and mouth incised. Down the center were five bold flying-fox designs, surrounded by shell-nosepiece and cuscus-tail motifs. The outer rim was also

81

incised with cuscus-tail symbols. The shield was painted with white lime, red ocher, and black soot.

Everyone stood up to examine the shield. Leo turned it this way and that way. The men talked to one another while they looked and looked. Leo shook his head: "Aduh! I do not know. It is a good shield. I like the way it is carved. Aduh! Is it from Sawa or from Erma? Is it from Weo or As-Atat?" He shook his head as if there were something about the shield that spoke directly to him, but he said nothing. They were all bewildered. None of them recognized the shield's origin until Jokmenipitsj, one of the older men, called out, "It is from the hand of Leo Bini himself!"

Each of the men took a deep breath and whispered, "Aduh!" Leo picked up the shield again, shook his head, and shook it again. He did not recognize the shield he had carved so many years ago. In fact, he was astonished. Suddenly, it came back to him. He called out, "Djisiriwitsj! The shield was named for my elder brother, Djisiriwitsj, who was killed by the people of Sawa." Leo Bini felt that his brother was back among the living and was with us in the museum. "Djisiriwitsj," he whispered. "Djisiri-witsj," he wailed softly.

There is a vast difference in carvings made with metal and those made with bone and stone. The power and striking imagery of shields carved in the old manner are missing in the newer work, although a major part of this has been the result of carvers losing their spiritual interest in the carv-ings. In the past, all artifacts—shields, drums, spears, figures—were the embodiment of those for whom they were named. The carvings, therefore, had meaning and were very much alive. They had a spirituality and inten-sity that is neither seen nor felt in later carvings. Most, if not all, present-day carvings are made for sale, many of them hacked out overnight when the carvers and even noncarvers hear that tourists are about to arrive. Rit-ual carvings, too, are now being offered for sale, although, traditionally, many of them would have been taken into the forest after use, broken up to release the spirits, and left in the stands of sago palms for the spirits to protect and nourish the trees. Today, newer works are scaled down in size for easy packing and shipping. The Asmat are wonderfully adaptive and do not hesitate to change the conception of a ritual carving if they think it will help sell the object.

The oldest shield in the Rijksmuseum voor Volkerkunde in Leiden, dated 1906, was carved with metal tools and has great beauty. It is well proportioned, smoothly and sharply carved, and elegant in design, with a basic pattern of the shell nosepiece, the *bipane* design. Yet it lacks the char-acter of the shields collected a year later on the Unir and Lorentz Rivers, where the men were still using only stone and bone and shell carving tools. The most obvious difference is in the texture of the carving. The rough, bold quality of the shields gives them an excitement and fierceness not found in pieces made with metal tools. The main designs on the shields of that time were not always centered; they were, however, always perfectly balanced. A startling energy emanated from them; they had the vigor and passion of what we in the West think of as Art. The earliest figure carvings in Leiden also appear to have been carved with stone and bone; they, too, have a power and boldness not evident in later works.

Carvers like Fai, also of Jamasj, were always ready to carve and to talk. Fai was an old man, or so he seemed to me. He stumbled and slipped as he walked naked along the muddy path from his home to the men's house. He shuffled along rather than walked. It was not possible to say how old he was. He may have been sixty, although he looked more like seventy or seventy-five. He had bright, light red scraggly hair that was uncombed and seemed to fly out in all directions. The flesh of his narrow abdomen hung in folds and creases. His skin had yellowed to almost the color of the hair on his head. He looked vaguely like an albino. His back was bent so that his chest appeared to be hollow. His limbs, all four of them, were like sticks, all bone, no flesh. Yet he would sit on the floor of the men's house and carve for four or five hours at a time, putting his tool down every twenty minutes or so and lying down for a minute or two to rest. He was working on one of the spirit figures of a *wuramon*, a soulship that would be the centerpiece of an initiation ceremony to take place in three or four months. He was carving one of the spirit figures. The *wuramon* would help the initiates cross the void between the world of childhood and the world of adulthood, the world of warriors. The young would move from this life into another.

The young initiates are about eleven or twelve years old. Boys are initiated on one day and girls on another. Both sexes have the same very simple design carved on chest or back. The boys line up and crawl over the turtle figure in the center of the soulship, symbolic of both fertility and virility because of the large number of eggs it lays. They crawl over the *wuramon* and then are scarified.

Fai worked alone on one end of the huge artifact. He still carved with a nail chisel, rather than a store-bought one, and used a stone ax without a handle as his mallet. In long strides, I measured the soulship to be thirty-three feet long. The carving had eleven spirit beings, each one worked on by a single carver. All the spirits were named after someone recently dead, so they all had individual names. There were spirits that lived at the bottom of the river, where there are whirlpools, and there were human spirits. There was a turtle in the center. There was an *okom*, a Z-shaped figure, that also lived in whirlpools. Two of these bottomless canoes were launched at the same time. That is, they were taken outside to the edge of the river, amid great hullabaloo, and placed on racks of the bone house in which the initiates had stayed temporarily.

Fai was one of the eleven carvers working on the piece, one of the rare carvings that could be worked on by more than one person at a time. I asked, "Fai, do you remember the days when you carved with stone tools, with bone and with shell?" He cupped his ear to hear me better. After I repeated my question, he said, "Oh, it was a long time ago."

Fai began to cough. When he recovered he went on: "I hardly remember those years. We carved with shells and with bones. I do not know what kind of shell they used. I know that I used the same shell that my father's father used."

I never saw one of those carving shells in Asmat, but assume from other New Guinea cultures that it was a tridacna, a clamshell that can grow to a huge size. The Asmat use bailer shells for bailing the water out of canoes. There were also the *Syrinx aruanus* shells, which were worn at the waist by important headhunters and their wives.

"The leg bones of a cassowary were particularly good as chisels," Fai added. He began to cough again. He lay back, turned onto his stomach, and spread two sections of sago spathe that he used to sit on and pissed between them onto the ground. He sat up and looked out at the Unir River as though to gather his thoughts.

"Yes," he said. "They were good days, but now the carving goes faster. Now, we have metal tools. We have knives to cut wood and axes to cut down trees. I like the new chisels. They make carving so much easier."

I watched Fai work. I listened to the chucking of the chisel when his right hand hit the wood of the handle, and I listened to the clopping of the stone ax when it struck the chisel. Wooden chips dropped easily into Fai's lap or flew into the air and fell to the floor. Sometimes the look on his face was wistful, as though he were thinking of other times, when head-hunting was still part of daily life. I, too, reminisced, as though I, too, had often taken part in Asmat battles.

My journal, of course, was always with me. I wanted to record everything, but a day never went by when I did not forget something important. Adults and children watched me write, but I could not concentrate when surrounded by a noisy crowd. I wanted to make sure that my judgment was clear, particularly when it came to my thoughts on the deterioration in the quality of the carvings. I might be reaching a point where I was not completely honest with myself.

Was I discriminating against the new? Was I prejudging with my brain rather than with my eye and what I think of as my intuitive sense of what art is, what is good and right? Was I assuming that old is most often good; new, most often bad?

Change

Take a look at the two great works of art just inside the entranceway of the Roman Catholic cathedral in Agats. There are two huge, stunningly incised and carved tree trunks, perhaps twenty feet tall. The work is superb. The trees, stripped of bark, radiate such elegance and power that they leave a glow inside the viewer. They are so intensely spiritual in feeling, as well as sensual, that I always want to hug them, to run my hands over the smooth surface. They were carved six or seven years ago, hardly old from anyone's point of view. Yet there is an indefinable, vague element in them of what we think of when we recognize an important creation.

Take another look at the weird and beautiful carving in the museum in Agats that was given to the bishop by a carver from Damen. It is simple, perhaps simple-minded. It is of a whole new category of carving in Asmat, an openwork wall hanging. It is of wood with six pairs of nude male figures seen from the rear, climbing a ladder, two men to a rung. On each side, there is a snake that helps frame the piece and holds it together. It is painted red, white, and black. I do not know the story behind the work, but it is obviously an allegory based on an Asmat myth. It is a work that could happily hang in any art museum in the world and was made in 1993.

Here is what I wrote in my journal during those days:

To retain its value and strength, art must be in constant change; it must continuously evolve or degenerate into decorative craftsmanship. The art of Asmat has, in many cases, remained faithful to the spirit of the past, changing only within the limits of its own culture. In some cases, the work has been corrupted under the influence of outsiders primarily seeking to make the artifacts more salable, thus bringing about a true cash economy. It was never anyone's intention to disturb the individuality of the carvers, only to make the carvings more accessible to the tourist.

Changes that come through the creative spirit of a carver are part of the system of inner stimulation that makes for Art; changes that come about through the direct interference of outsiders, no matter how well-intentioned, have little or nothing to do with creativity and can be harmful—assuming one wants to retain the creative aspect. The old style figures do not sell as well as the new.

This is not to challenge ideas that come from foreign cultures as being less than fruitful, whether they come from the West or from societies like that of the Asmat. The carvers themselves were never interested in making what we think of as works of Art, a concept that was foreign to them until recently. They were making objects that were the embodiment of their ancestors, ritual carvings that were necessary to their celebrations and vengeful feelings. The carvers never thought of themselves as artists. They were carvers, master craftsmen. The larger the work, the less chance there would be for selling it. The more refined the work, the more likely it will sell. Figure carvings that have been blackened with pig fat or

Change

fish fat to make them appear to have been used in ritual life, sell. Erotic works sell. Drums sell, shields sell, the smaller the better since they are easier to carry. The phallic projection of ancestor poles has been folded up into the uppermost figure so that the pole can easily be rolled in bubblewrap on board the ship or more easily slipped into the Cessna.

To date, outside influence on the carvings has been negative in my eyes, as far as its artistic quality is concerned. A carving contest sponsored each year by the museum in Agats was a brilliant idea, but has motivated carvers to work only in one single style, the style that wins prizes and is quickly bought up by foreigners for relatively high prices. The bishop is now changing the categories of the contest, giving prizes to the best creative ideas, the most beautiful shield or drum; in fact, in several different classifications. I trust this will allow the carvers new ways of showing their creativity.

No society can remain static once the outside world has visited it. Asmat has gained with this contact to the extent that almost all carvings have become objects for sale. This has allowed the Asmat to buy clothing, tobacco, canned foods, axes, knives, fishing gear, and other Western artifacts that had never been part of their culture. There had never been a need for these artifacts of the West. Men lived naked except for body decoration—paint, nosepieces, necklaces, dance belts, cuscus headbands studded with white feathers. Women wore only a girdle made of sago leaves, in addition to the same kind of decorations the men wore. Now, except for church-going, most Asmat wear clothing so ragged the people look poverty-stricken, which they are not, money in hand or not. They eat rice now as well as sago at feasts, a food product they must pay for, although the Indonesian government subsidizes it. In times past, they ate only food found in the forest and rivers and the sea.

The museum in Agats has been the recipient of a major donation from Freeport McMoRan of New Orleans. Freeport owns the huge gold and copper mine in Tembagapura, northwest of Asmat. Some of this money was used to make renovations of what used to be the storage wing of the museum, turning it into a grand Display Room for traditional works. The Education Room which had housed the only free library in all of Indonesia was emptied of its books, magazines and newspapers, its tables and chairs, and all the paraphernalia for showing slides and films of Charlie Chaplin and Laurel and Hardy. The original purpose of the museum had been to give the Asmat a sense of his own worth, his own identity, and an understanding of the rituals of headhunting and cannibalism. It was meant to be a place where the children could learn the history of their past and not be degraded by those who looked down on them because they could not read or write and walked around naked. Now, the museum serves a different purpose, an audience of sophisticated, relatively rich Germans, Americans, Dutch, Italians, Frenchmen, Scandinavians and other Europeans.

My objections have nothing to do with accepting what the Asmat carvers are

86

Change

doing today, but in giving the attention to it in the museum that it does not deserve, raising it to the level of the older works that are there. Simply by devoting a whole room to the new carvings, for me, is unfair to the carvings and to all who go to Asmat to learn of their traditions.

If you look at carvings made 80 or 90 years ago, works that are in Leiden, in Basle, in London and elsewhere in Europe, it becomes obvious that there has been a steady decline in the carvings as works of Art. The artistic quality of the carvings, except for artifacts made for traditional rituals, has declined into airport art. Superb ritual works are still being made, although the feasts themselves have changed from the traditional to those celebrating Christmas, Easter, and Indonesian Independence.

7

Biwiripitsj

Have you ever been old? Have you ever reached out with wrinkled fingers and wrinkled hands to touch the tender skin of youth? Memories, real and unreal, flood my veins, forcing me to think back to my own spare youth, when I had seen no naked flesh other than my own. I had never run a hand over a breast with pointed nipples stiffening, never touched an abdomen in which the navel, Center of the Universe, lies. In my old age, almost everyone is young, younger than myself. In Asmat, men and women age early, are already old at forty. I see now how mistaken I was to think of forty as being old, for when I was in my teens, it seemed ancient, as it did to all the young.

In Asmat, when I looked at Biwiripitsj that first time I went upstream to his village and saw him naked in church, not only was his body bared, but his soul was as well. He had been named after one of the great ancestors, a mythological hero, Biwiripitsj, who had been instrumental in telling all Asmat the ways of warfare and cannibalism.

Even though old, even though forty, he revealed silken flesh to all the world as though he were clothed in thick garments of fleece from which electrical charges flew from wool to skin, from skin to wool, sending sparks around his body. His hands were lifted to his waist and were cupped in front of him as he stood in the slow-moving line to receive the Eucharist from Father Johnny Fleischhacker. He wore a beatific smile that I could not interpret. When he accepted the wafer and put it into his mouth, was he thinking of the flesh of mankind or of the men and women he had killed in vengeance? Was he ingesting the spirit of the whole of Asmat? Was he thinking of swallowing Jesus himself when that Eucharist dissolved inside him? Would the body of Christ give him the same physical strength as the actual flesh of his decapitated enemy? No wine was offered, but he might have been transubstantiating some imaginary form of alcohol into blood, transmuting the water into flesh. Was one more real to him than the other? He was standing in the aisle in utter silence, his humility transcending pride and arrogance. What had he substituted for the cannibalized flesh of human enemies? What was substituted inside him for that need to prove himself the warrior great enough to take four heads, to go into battle and kill an enemy? He stood there approaching the pastor in a gesture sublime and eloquent, sublime and fierce, for he was about to eat that wafer of human flesh.

Biwiripitsj was not old, not young; he was the essence of Man, not Mankind, as he stood there, beads of sweat dripping from his forehead, from his chest and back. He exuded strength and power. He exuded the smells of the forest, rank and unpleasant, which came from dead leaves, dead insects, and animals, mixed with mud and peat bog and the perspiration of those standing or sitting in pews. The sweat seemed to drip from the roof of the church itself, dropping onto everyone, each of the parishioners enveloped within it. Everyone was old, everyone young, for they have existed throughout the millennia of humans on earth.

Have you ever been old? Have you ever touched that wondrous flesh of a man or a woman so young that he or she might be no more than twenty-five and you no less than seven and seventy? Biwiripistj might have allowed me to reach back into history, into his own history, to a time when the man for whom he was named lived with his brother Desoipitsj, who was demanding a human head that would teach the Asmat the ways of warfare. Biwiripitsj listened to his brother, cut off his sibling's head with a bamboo knife, and pinned it to the floor of their house. It was then that the voice of Desoipitsj came from the decapitated head, telling Biwiripitsj how to butcher his body, how it was necessary for him and all Asmat to follow his exact instructions so that the spirit world would not descend upon them and destroy all life. Vengeance was necessary to their way of life. They must protect themselves, their wives, their children, and their sago. Desoipitsj and Biwiripitsj taught the Asmat warfare and retribution against all who take their fish and their sago trees.

This new, young human named Biwiripitsj was close in front of me, his body wet and erotic as he stood in that church, as if he stood inside a universe of Asmat myth, a solitary figure who had conquered enemies and brought home heads. He took me back to a time in his life, now long gone, when violence and pain and death were part of daily existence and necessary to the search for courage and vengeance. I had not lived in the time of Biwiripitsj's elders and had never experienced the great physical pain that great warriors had suffered. It was Biwiripitsj and his cohorts who had listened and turned from warfare to peace to the acceptance of the wafer instead of human flesh. That dire need for vengeance—where had it gone? What exchange had taken place to relieve him of obligations to his ancestors? What replacement had allowed him to forget the early training, that induced him to give up one spiritual life for another, a different spirituality?

Everyone in Asmat was ready to stop the warfare and the cannibalism. It ended easily, quickly. There were no repercussions. Christ had taken on the burden of vengeance. The Asmat need no longer think about it.

I had no answers then for anyone looking for the way to freedom, the escape route from the real world of spirits. I have no answers now that are not my own secrets. On occasion, I know the relevant questions, but, more often than not, there are no answers. We are all connected through the universe, but we are separated here on earth, living with our families behind the closed walls of the forest and trying to find some belief system, be it through some esoteric Buddhist cult or through the animistic rites of Asmat.

I am always in the midst of that dilemma. The spirits lurk in the whirlpools at the bends of rivers, always hidden but sometimes bursting out in anger at a negligent soul for its lack of attention to the proper ceremonial rites for the dead. It is then that the spirits get angry. It is then that the drought comes, that the fish disappear and the food is gone. In the past, there was always time for vengeance against enemy villages. But now, Christ is there, taking upon himself that need to avenge all deaths.

I have never fallen by the wayside. I have never failed to approach at least part of what I was looking for, the part most germane to the world of the spirits, the need for vengeance in order to free all ancestors from the land of the living, giving them the freedom to go on to the Land of the Dead. I do not know whether I ever entered into practices that might be deemed controversial. I suppose I have. I must have gone on some forbidden path at some point in my life, but remain unaware of its effects on me. If I could steal the life spirit of Biwiripitsj, I would accept it into my own physical body, for I remain in the midst of a potent Asmat religion concerning spirits and spirituality, and suddenly see Biwiripitsj in a different guise, as one whose spiritual attitude recognizes the existence of supernatural powers, believing it so thoroughly that I must believe it myself. I do not understand what I see of him on the surface, what he shows to the world. Has he truly accepted Christianity, Christ on the Cross, the Resurrection? Was he always destined to be a warrior, to kill and be killed? Was his destiny to become Christian? Was his destiny to carve works of art that were spiritual even under the influence of outsiders?

I think of the three works in the museum in Agats carved by Koko-putsj. The serenity of these sculptures should be enough to convert the most recalcitrant believer or nonbeliever. In fact, I visualize Biwiripitsj seated on a bench as he now sits, his hands in his lap, fingers interlaced, the remains of the wafer still melting in his mouth. He is the centerpiece of a sculpture of a group of men, not as Christ himself but as part of his cir-cle. He is confident; he is diffident; he is whole. He combines the truth with the untruths of his beliefs and gives off an aura of acceptance with which I identify.

I have never been tempted, when I left a friend, a lover, a people, to leave anything of myself behind but the excretions of my body. No books, no clothes, no food. I was always taking myself away, separating myself from friends and living in my own world, just when fullest, closest contact was being made, just when it would have been possible to make some per-manent connection, when life was saying, "Hey! You got this far. You can rest easy now."

But I could never rest, even that time in Father Frank Trenkenschuh's village of Ayam, when he was so sympathetic and understanding of me and my way of life. It was the occasion for blessing and opening the new church and a new men's house. I was trying to be at peace within myself. It must have been 3:30 in the morning. I was closing my eyes to keep out the physical images in front of me. The blessing would take place tomor-row when the bishop arrived from Agats with his long reed full of *mbi,* the magical white powder that protected all under its spell and blinded the en-emy. The bishop would toss the *mbi* at the walls, inside and outside, thus killing all the remaining spirits that were up to no good. The *mbi* is made of burned, crushed mussel shells, most often used as white paint.

Night was the time of spirits. The ceremonies taking place were only the beginnings of the rituals that would last until the following evening. The men's house was packed with men carrying torches. They yelped and chanted and chased out spirits. They were terrifying those that lingered there within the nipa leaves of the walls. They poked their flaming torches into all the cracks and crevices, everywhere a spirit might hide. Surely, nothing could survive that reign of terror against them. There was the smell of sorcery in the night, of dried leaves burning as the torches swiped the leaves of the walls, the sense of supernatural powers enveloping the en-tire village.

I was lying on the floor of the men's house, my head on my blow-up pil-low, a sarong around my waist. Suddenly there was loud shouting, and everyone was rushing outside. Trenk's voice came to me, calling me to get off my sleeping mat and go out into the darkness. I stood with hundreds of men and women watching the scene from the bank of the Asewetsj River. There was a gibbous moon shining, giving us all a good view of the spirit approaching from the other side of the river. I was getting the shivers. The whole night was of dreams, of spells and charms, of sorcery. Surely, everyone could hear my heart pounding. We stood in the darkness, eyes riveted on the spirit standing in the middle of the dugout. Two paddlers in the canoe, one fore, one aft, were directing the dugout to the muddy riverbank. There might have been dead silence. Everyone was tense with the excitement of watching the spirit moving slowly from the blackness of night to the river. If there was any shouting or yelping, I did not hear it. Like all 2,000 people of Ayam, I was transfixed by the spirit's image, which was almost floating on the sky reflected in the still river, the water itself throwing back light There is no question that the Asmat were determined to drive all evil, all illness from the village.

When the dugout arrived, hundreds of children were on the riverbank, ready to chase the spirit out of the village. The spirit was easily recognized. It was a body mask, with the top half a rattan basket turned upside down that covered the head and upper body, and the lower half a skirt made of shredded sago leaves. The children threw rotting fruit and mud at the spirit and then chased it around the village and into the jungle. Some minutes later, the spirit reappeared, only to be driven out again. Finally, at dawn, it was chased one last time, taking with it all the harmful spirits that were still hiding around the village.

Ancestor poles being raised, Bajun Village, 1978

Ancestor poles being carried out of the men's house, Buepis Village, 1979

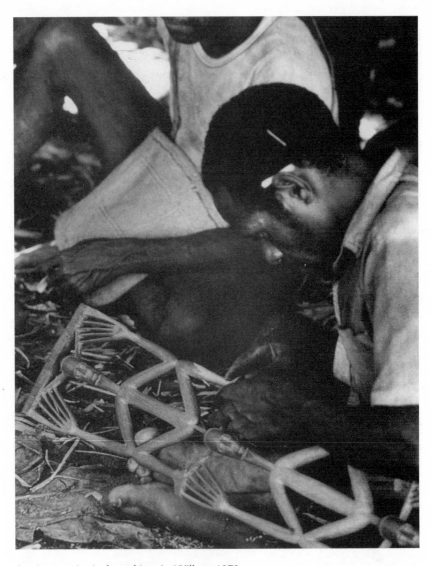

An ajour carving in the making, Atsj Village, 1978

Shields being carved, Jamasj Village, 1978

The gunwale of a canoe being incised with magical symbols, Jamasj Village, 1978

A soulship being carried out of the men's house, Jamasj Village, 1978

Initiates waiting in isolation before an adoption ceremony, Pirien Village, 1978

Men in a mud free-for-all, Otsjenep Village, 1979

A Kombai shield, Amarou Village, 1979

A woman from Tajan Village, 1979

A man from Surabi Village, 1979

8

The *Djuwus* and the *Ndamup*

Early in November 1993, I returned to New York after two months in Indonesia. David Vereano had died; Stephen had died; Darryl was in St. Vincent's at the end of his short stay on earth; and Sam was in St. Vincent's, too, at the end of *his* time. Both Darryl and Sam had cytomegalovirus, microbacterial avian infection, Kaposi's sarcoma, you name it. It wasn't an easy time for anyone, not for lovers of the sick, not for their friends, least of all for those with AIDS. It suddenly seemed as though there were more deaths from AIDS than in any previous year of the plague. It is true of my friends, so many dying, so many discovering they are HIV positive. Coincidence, perhaps, but too many deaths have piled up this year, and I cannot get out of my mind the article in the *New York Times* on the young gays of San Francisco who watch their friends die, feel guilty about their own survival, and, in some form or another of suicide, are going back to their old ways of anal intercourse without condoms.

I have friends other than young ones, of course. Dorle was ninety-three in the year of 1993, bless her; Mildred was eighty-seven; Francis was somewhere in his late eighties; and Joe had just announced that he was eighty-five, God bless them all. I was a youngster at seventy-two.

I was with Dorle on an afternoon excursion to the School of American Ballet. We had been invited by Curtis Harnack to watch class. Curtis was then head of the school. While we stood greeting one another, Danilova walked in wearing a great fur coat. She was with a companion. She came

101

over and talked to Dorle and Curt. She brought with her an entourage of sweet fragrances. I was meeting her for the first time and was like a child meeting a princess or King Arthur. Danilova was then ninety-two, a year younger than Dorle. After a few minutes, Danilova went off to teach class while the three of us went into Curt's office. We stood there, smiling at one another with the pleasure of having just talked to Danilova, one of the greatest dancers of all time. Dorle grinned and almost glowed with pride "Oh, my," she said. "Just look at her. She looks so old!"

Dorle has no pain, she says, no arthritis, no Parkinson's. Certainly, there is no loss of memory of the past, although her hearing and sight are less than perfect and continue to deteriorate. She still loves gossip, still loves to tell stories of the time she worked in publicity for the New York Philharmonic in the 1930s: "Maestro [Toscanini] used to call me up at one or two o'clock in the morning, every morning. He never slept. He would call and say, 'Dorle, my sweet, I love you.' I would say, 'I love you too, Maestro.' Then I would bang the receiver down and go right back to sleep."

Dorle, Francis, Joe, and Mildred were still going to the opera, to the theater, and out to dinners that year, still inviting others as guests and having parties of their own. It encourages me, inspires me, to watch them enjoy their lives. They all have that look of dignity that we of a younger generation have not yet attained. I have the aches and pains of old age, but I have not achieved that august appearance and carriage I so admire, and almost certainly never will. I have, however, maintained the family tradition of having had an operation for colon cancer, three hip-replacement surgeries on one hip, a gallbladder removal, and even a TURP, or transurethral prostate operation, in the lower portion of my body, aside from my having recently learned that I have Parkinson's disease. Of course, my older friends might have physical problems, but I do not see them, either because I choose not to do so or because they choose not to reveal them. The exterior of their lives is energetic and fulfilling: *Death in Venice* at the Metropolitan one night, a Charles Ludlam play two nights later.

I continually learn from friends, old and young, longtime friends and new friends, and I see that the young are so young! Sam at forty-four was probably the oldest to die this year, with David at forty-three, Stephen somewhere in his thirties, and Darryl at twenty-eight. None had reached his forty-fifth birthday, the year in which most men's mid-life crises begin to devastate them emotionally. My own mid-life crisis came at the age of fifty, but it was not a negative one at all. It was, in fact, the reverse of negative. It was my most wonderful year, when everything was looking up instead of down, when everything in my life seemed to come together, when I felt fulfilled and satisfied. Not only was that year a good one, but each successive year has been better. I don't mind getting older—at least, for the moment.

It was during my fiftieth year that I began to realize that my feelings of being unattractive were simply a matter of an image in my own mind that probably had nothing to do with reality. My friends saw me through their own eyes and minds, while I looked in the mirror and saw only the surface reflected back. The truth is that I will always see myself as homely, but I have come to realize that not all others see me in the same way. It always startles me to hear Floriano reminisce about his own early life in Rome, when he thought himself plain and undesirable. This, from a man whose remarkable beauty is both interior and exterior and has been so all his life. I do not know what happened during that fiftieth year to give me new life, to turn me around, away from my periodic depressions, replacing them with stimulation, passion, excitement. Is it just that time passes and normal healing takes place? Or is it that sometimes some of us do learn? Somehow, I feel that I learned to accept whoever I am, for the good or the bad.

Now, watching the young die, watching the elderly live, compels a certain amount of rumination and meditation within me. I had not had much success in finding a permanent partner, but that no longer bothered me. I preferred the far half of my bed to be empty when I woke up in the morning. It was rare that I would ask anyone to spend the night, perhaps once a year or once every two years. Often enough, I had a young friend who came to dinner and seemed to enjoy sexual pleasures before he left. In some ways, it might even be to my advantage to be physically unattractive. I knew that I was not being approached simply for having a pretty face or for the influence I might or might not have. Being alone meant I could get up as usual at six o'clock in the morning, shower, have my shredded wheat while reading the *New York Times,* and then get to work on whatever I was doing, with no distractions.

The persistent image of Sam dead, with me standing at his bedside, with Gerald, his lover, looking down, conjures up like a shot the whole of my past in Asmat. Bang-o! it is there, for Sam's body lay on his bed, his head slightly akilter, his body akilter, too. His mouth was open, and he looked as though he were staring in awe at some distant happening or into the new world of peace he was entering. His body lay exactly as I remember the body of a woman in Asmat having lain on a pandanus mat, her head akilter, her body akilter, her mouth open, her eyes open, not yet dead but the family wailing inside the house and out. They are wailing her to death, I thought. She could no longer return to the land of the living. She heard the wailing and realized that they were keening for *her* and that death was imminent, if it was not already upon her. She might even wonder whether she was already a spirit, a *djuwus.* The attack of malaria had pushed her over the edge of despair, and the wailing had taken her closer to death. She awaited the transformation of her spirits into the one life spirit that would allow her to begin her journey to the Land of the Dead. No one had sought out the pastor for chloroquine. No one had seemed to want to bring her meandering spirit back into its body, back into the world of the living. The family already had accepted her death, although the women closest to her had not yet taken off their skirts and rolled naked in the mud. Nor had their heads been shaved. That would come when the breathing stopped. Death was an almost constant companion of the living. Men, women, and children most often die of complications during a bout of malaria. A spirit had taken possession of this woman, and the family members thought that they could do nothing to help. They felt, in truth, that they should do nothing about reviving her. People die quickly in Asmat, no hanging around for weeks or months. No hospital visits once a day or twice a week. The Asmat have an instinct about death and hurry it along with their plaintive cry and howl.

The dead in Asmat have a relatively easy time of it. It is their spirits that control the lives of the living. They easily spread a few deaths around the village, warning everyone of their demands for vengeance. In the past, the family would have gone off on a raid within weeks or months of the death and brought back a decapitated head or two. The spirit of an ancestor could destroy the family, devastate the village. Or it could bring good luck to all, give them power over all enemies, enrich the stands of sago, fill the rivers with fish. It could lie in wait until an enemy slept and his spirit wandered through the night; it could enter the enemy's empty body, take possession of it, and play havoc there—a veritable dybbuk.

Spirits inhabit the land of the living as well as the Land of the Dead. Not all are spirits of human beings. There are spirits that dwell in the forest, in trees, in swamp waters, in streams, in animals, in the sun. *Ambirak* and *okom* spirits, both crustaceans, probably live only in the northwest, within a limited area of Asmat, swimming at the bottom of whirlpools at the bends of rivers. Neither has ever been fully described. They are carved with a series of other spirits in soulships during initiation ceremonies. They travel in a bottomless canoe, the only spirits that may do so. They must be spirits so related to each other that they are permitted to paddle within the same canoe.

Human spirits may enter and reside within a living body. Everyone, in fact, has two spirits: the *ndamup*, which roams the village and forest, usually at night, when its living body is asleep; and the *djuwus*, which leaves the body permanently only at death. The Asmat often talk about spirits; they are everywhere and are ever-present, personalized, recognizable, inevitably triumphant. At night, no one may step over the body of a sleeping man or woman, for the *ndamup* will never find its way home again.

"It will happen," said Leo Bini in Jamasj one day, "that the village of

Sawa [traditional enemy of Jamasj] will capture a man of Jamasj, will kill him, and will eat him. In spite of this, his *djuwus,* his spirit, returns to Jamasj and lives a normal life with his family. Even he himself does not know he is dead. Sometimes he lifts something very heavy, and his body begins to bleed. He may have no sores or cuts, but he bleeds from his body. The people might then look at him and at the blood and say, 'Oh! He is dead. He has been killed already.' If he hears this, he will surely die. Or maybe at night, when everyone is asleep, his arms come apart, his legs come apart, his head comes off, just the way they killed him in Sawa, just the way our ancestor Desoipitsj said we must cut up the bodies of our enemies. Everyone can see this, but they pretend not to see. They do not want him to know what they see. In the morning, all the parts go back together.

"Vincent Ojak's father, Josep Osep, was a *djuwus* who was killed in Sorong and came home to Jamasj. A human being can live a long time as a *djuwus,* unless someone suddenly says to him, 'You are a *djuwus!*' If this is said, the man will die right away. He has no idea that he is a *djuwus.* When he dies, his death is like that of other men.

"Now, the *ndat djuwus* is the spirit of life force. It may roam at will if it is an enemy. If the *ndat djuwus* comes from Jufri in the night, it means that its owner will be killed in the next battle. When a canoe is almost finished, it is sprinkled with *mbi,* white lime made from mussel shells. The power of the *mbi* will force the *ndat ndamup* to sit up in the front of the canoe during a battle. The spirit is a small being. When *mbi* is thrown over new canoes or new men's houses, the men shout, 'Go away *djuwus!* Go away sickness! Go away *ndamup!*' In this way, the spirit cannot do harm to the owners of the canoe. If this spirit is killed, its owner will die immediately, no matter how far away he is."

The *djuwus* leaves the body when a person is ill and returns when the person is again in good health. Its return to the body means a return to good health. When it stays away, it means death, just like the *djuwus* that refused to return to the body of the woman I watched die. If a person is destined to be killed shortly, the life force leaves the body in advance.

In Jufri, Kosmos Mbap said, "It is not only men who have *ndamup* and *djuwus* spirits. Women and children have them, too.

"When I go into the jungle to hunt birds, it may be that I will meet my friend Komor even though he is really at home. He may be at home, sleeping or eating, or out fishing. But I meet him, and we have some talk. It doesn't matter about what. Then we go our separate ways. Later, when I go home, there is Komor in his house in the village. This is the real Komor. The one I met in the forest is the *ndamup*. There are both good and bad *ndamup*. The spirit is separate from the man as if he were two real people."

It is the same as bilocation, I said to myself when I first heard of this ability to be in two different places at the same time. I believe it. I, too, feel a sense of bilocation at times in a bed in New York, on a mat in Asmat. I am in both places, loving my friends, visiting them, going on walks, enjoying the pleasures of both parts of the world and of my life, both at the same time.

"Sometimes," Kosmos Mbap went on, "the young do not treat the old people properly. They do not give them enough food. Sometimes a young *ndamup* will beat up an old man if there is provocation, if he does not share a particularly delicious piece of fruit or meat. If the young one meets the *ndamup* of the old person like Komor, Komor might beat him severely, maybe so badly, the young person will die. A man is never aware of what his *ndamup* is doing.

"If Komor and Titus are in the jungle and meet Kosmos Mbap's *ndamup,* all three will sit a while and will tell stories, or they might all even hunt together. Then they part. Back in the village, Komor and Titus go to the house of Kosmos Mbap and ask for sago. As guests, they expect to be given food. The Kosmos Mbap who is in the village at the time does not know that they have just been talking to his *ndamup* in the forest. At that moment, the *ndamup* might be inside the real man, or it might be roaming somewhere. If they tell the man they have seen his *ndamup,* Kosmos Mbap might die right then, just as it would happen with a *djuwus.* In olden times, there were many *ndamup.* Now there are few. Everyone used to have one of both kinds of spirits, but now with religion and outsiders, there aren't so many."

The *djuwus* and the *ndamup* are too confusing for me to understand their similar but distinct qualities. At times, they appear to be the same; at other times, they are vastly different. The Asmat help that confusion along in typical Asmat fashion by giving several explanations, all of which are true for them at the moment, even though to us they may contradict or duplicate one another.

Sam, of course, would have delighted in confusing us all even further. Now, which of Sam's spirits, his *ndamup* or his *djuwus,* is wandering our world at this moment? I would not be surprised if he switched from one to the other. He always had a playful side and would have loved to bedevil us in this way. So, too, would David, Stephen, and Darryl. They are all biding their time and will appear before us demanding vengeance, demanding our taking a head for each of them. It might be that Sam and Stephen, David and Darryl have all met in some gay bar in the netherworld and will gang up on us, scare us with their spirits, and demand a great celebration. I'm all for it.

9

Ancestor Spirits

The Asmat believe that wood chips from a canoe in the process of being carved may not be used to make fire, for the burning chips would drain the energy from the canoe, destroying the spirits therein and eliminating their protection.

In the village of Djakapis, far up the Jerep River, a man was so angry at the spirit within his shield that he smashed the shield, thereby sending the spirit forever to the Land of the Dead, never again to return to the land of the living. The spirit would no longer give him strength in battle or guard him from malevolent spirits or from humans out to kill him. Living human beings must be careful to understand and listen to the needs and desires of those in the spirit world, just as they must understand the same beings when they were alive, when they were still flesh and blood.

It was never easy to understand Asmat thinking. The spirit world dominated Asmat lives, often leading them into sorcery and warfare. In certain regions of Asmat, an ancestor-pole feast was held to memorialize those whose deaths had not yet been avenged. This ceremony included the naming of specific individuals carved on the pole whose spirits were demanding vengeance. Spirits indicated their displeasure by bringing sickness into the village, by killing off an inordinate number of babies in childbirth, or by performing any of a number of other acts, including the disappearance of fish from the sea and rivers. The spirits of those named on the pole were always impatient to be released from their obligations to tend to the living until their deaths were avenged. Then, and only then, could a spirit move to the Land of the Dead.

Part of an ancestor-pole feast took place during the celebration of the Year of Indonesia at the American Museum of Natural History in June 1991. I had been asked by the Asmat Progress and Development Foundation of Jakarta to curate a program of dances and demonstrations of carving techniques. A number of cities were mentioned as possible venues for this event, but only the Smithsonian Institution in Washington, the American Museum of Natural History in New York, the Field Museum in Chicago, and the New Orleans Museum of Art were on the final list. The time the Asmat had in the United States was limited by their visas, which permitted them only three weeks. I did not travel with them.

This project allowed me to return to Asmat to choose the group of men and women who would be visiting the United States. I knew that it would be difficult to find women who would be willing to participate, and, indeed, only one woman was not too frightened of the idea and really wanted to go. She was a widow named Marta Atnasaap, a thin woman with loose flesh around her breasts and waist. She was somewhere between thirty-five and forty, not very attractive but an energetic dancer who pleased everyone. There were twenty-eight men. In Asmat, I went to various villages looking for carvers and dancers, none of whom had ever been out of Asmat, let alone traveled to Europe or the United States. In truth, only a couple of handfuls of men had ever gone as far as the high school in Jayapura, on the northern coast of the island of New Guinea, about 300 miles from Asmat.

I talked to those making the trip about the problems they faced, but my effort was superfluous since they were taken to Jakarta for orientation a week before their scheduled flight. There, the foundation bought clothing for them and showed them the ways of toilets and showers, elevators and automobiles, electric-light switches and refrigerators.

Their schedule took them to the Smithsonian first. By the time I met them at Kennedy Airport in New York, they were old hands at traveling by plane and by bus. None was in the least fearful of the great distance they were going or the distance, when flying, between the plane and the ground or was even curious about how an airplane worked, how it was able to fly. They accepted everything because the spirits of white people had strong magic and obviously could do anything. The idea of a crash would never have troubled them.

The group was put up at a Hasidic-owned hotel on the Upper West Side, three short blocks from the museum in which they would be performing. It had taken only one night in Washington for them to become aware of the pleasures of porn videotapes in hotels, and they had stayed up

108

late watching erotic films. They felt more comfortable sitting, eating, and sleeping on the floor rather than on chairs or beds. The idea of putting only one or two people into a room seemed ludicrous to the Asmat. They preferred packing themselves in, eight or ten to a room, leaving the empty rooms for storing the clothing and carvings they had brought. They usually kept their doors wide open. Some sat on the floor of the hallway; others sat just inside the rooms.

Food was served regularly, cooked for the most part at the Indonesian Consulate on the other side of Central Park. It invariably consisted of boiled or fried rice with meat or fish. The Asmat eat a lot and are normally demanding about getting enough sago. However, no one said anything about the absence of what they think of as their most important food. Sometimes, they ate in fast-food restaurants: hamburgers or fried chicken. They were given a relatively small amount of money for what extras they might need. They spent freely on running shoes and jeans and chinos from moderately elegant clothing stores and on transistor radios. No one told them about batteries. They were usually broke. The money was handled by the Indonesians who accompanied the group.

The day after the Asmat arrived in New York, the Indonesian Consulate threw a grand party in its elegant building on East Sixty-eighth Street. The Asmat did not know quite what was happening. They were asked to dance for about ten minutes, which they did awkwardly, still a bit nervous about the trip, not sure what was wanted of them in this strange building with its grand curving staircase. The Caucasian guests were in elegant clothing; the Asmat, in shorts and feather decorations.

The men and Marta (who had a room for herself, but did not sleep alone) complained to me about the sidewalks of New York being too hard on their feet, even when they were wearing their running shoes. For the first couple of days, they walked around the streets barefoot, but then found wearing the sneakers much easier on their feet. When they dressed at the hotel for performances, they painted themselves, put feathers in their hair, added necklaces and wrist- and leg bands, and then went out looking marvelously wild. New Yorkers appeared indifferent, barely giving them a cursory glance as they went by. However, as word got around the city that former cannibals were dancing and carving at the American Museum of Natural History, many of the same New Yorkers began standing in front of the hotel, waiting with their cameras handy for the Asmat to go in or come out. In the lobby, there was always a curious juxtaposition of the decorated Asmat rubbing shoulders with Hasidic men in black hats and long black coats, with ringlets dripping from their temples.

In the museum, the Asmat sat and worked on a low platform in the middle of the Hall of Birds of the World. It was not necessary for all the

Asmat to be at the museum at the same time. Usually, the men took turns carving, first making sure that there was always a minimum of seven or eight men carving at any particular period. The others might take a trip somewhere or simply sleep through the day or go shopping. But in the museum, the men carved and made a splendid impression on those who watched. Small groups of people might stay for an hour or more, talking to one of the carvers through an interpreter from the museum. There were lectures and demonstrations and performances in various rooms around the museum. Visitors returned again and again, watching the ever-changing ancestor pole. The pole was about fifteen feet tall, but was always lying flat while being worked on. It looked smaller then. It wasn't until the pole was finished and standing vertically that it had its most profound effect.

The first section to be carved was the phallic wing, which projected from the groin area of the uppermost figure. The wing, known as the penis, or *cemen,* of the pole, was one of the roots of a rhizophore, a type of mangrove with wedge roots, one of which is left intact when the tree is cut down in the forest. When turned upside down, carved, and decorated, it was a formidable object, with an astonishing spiritual quality. The Asmat had brought the tree trunk with them, from Irian Jaya. Most of the symbols carved on the trunk represented the decapitated heads of enemies; there were also the motifs of the *bipane,* the shell-nosepiece design that symbolizes the tusks of a wild boar. There were five figures on the pole, one above the other like a totem pole. Each of the five faces was grinning fiercely in a way that was meant to terrify those who looked at it, except for family members. In Asmat, only one carver at a time usually works on a pole. At the museum, two or three carvers worked simultaneously or worked on smaller artifacts. Others carved pieces they hoped to sell to the public.

It probably was Father Frank Trenkenschuh who had the idea of asking the Asmat to choreograph their own version of the Fumeripitsj creation myth. They quickly translated the myth into dance, acting it out with humor and intelligence. The beginning of the performance was easily staged, even with literally only ten minutes of rehearsal time. Fumeripitsj was on stage, carving male and female figures that later came to life and became the Asmat people. With the beating of the drums, the statues began to move, at first awkwardly, stiffly, jerking their bodies around, unable to stand, barely able to move. In coming to life, the statues were delightful, hilarious, full of ingenious creativity. The Asmat have a great talent for acting and have vivid imaginations. The staging was cleverly done, aside from the fact that the Asmat loved bringing in new action so that the whole of the dance was never the same, always different in one way or another.

There was something going on at the museum with the Asmat almost every minute of the ten days they were in New York. Some visitors attended every event and would not leave until after the Asmat themselves had left the platform for the hotel. The culmination ceremonies were saved for the last two days: a Saturday and Sunday.

Trenk and I were at the museum every day, making sure that there was no exploitation of any kind. The platform space was more than adequate. The carvers were comfortable, even though they could not smoke in the museum. The Hall of Birds of the World was huge, with glass cases in which were displayed birds and other animals. Even though it had no atmosphere of distant forestlands, the spirits of other cultures managed to filter into the great gallery and into the Asmat themselves. After two or three days, we all began to feel different, almost electrified by the atmosphere generated by the carvers and dancers. The Asmat were confused at first, unable to make a connection with whatever spirits might be there. Still, as the ancestor pole, the *bisj,* was being worked on and as other carvings were coming into reality, the spirits of those to be named began to hover around us. With each passing hour, with each group of visitors to come by, something extraordinary took place. After some days, there was an aliveness in the hall that surely had not been there before. Crowds of people had obviously made special trips with children and with other adults, aware that something unusual was going on. The spontaneous rapport between the audience and the performers was joyous and enthralled everyone.

The naming of those on the ancestor pole took place on Saturday afternoon, after the carving of the pole was finished. Most of the Asmat began working on the decorations, painting the entire pole and tying on embellishments of grasses found in Central Park. The drums were loud; the chanting was loud. It was like some rock opera in which the lyrics are impossible to understand.

Marta Atnasaap was suddenly in her element and did her star turn then, dancing what I call the cassowary, a simple movement, mostly a knocking of knees together and a flapping of hands and elbows, much like the flapping of the wings of the huge bird. The five drums the men had brought from Asmat were beaten, their sound reverberating through the halls. Marta began singing out the names and exploits of all those depicted on the pole, first calling out the name of her late husband and telling the glorious story of his glorious death. Each of the five figures carved on the pole was given the name of someone who recently had died. Marta then sang out the brave deeds that each had done.

The whole of the Asmat event ended spectacularly with a procession of men carrying the ancestor pole on their shoulders down to the Kaufmann

Theater, the main auditorium of the museum, where it was donated to the city of New York.

Early Sunday afternoon, the Asmat could be seen on their platform painting their faces and bodies black and red and white. Their hair was clustered with the white feathers of the yellow-crested cockatoo. One of the men was beating a drum slowly, chanting to himself. Other men were adjusting the cuscus-fur headband that all Asmat men and women wear or were putting on necklaces of dog teeth or were pushing armlets of two wild-boar tusks above the elbow: one pair of tusks a sign that the man wearing it had taken one head; two pairs, two heads; and so on.

The procession began with the men lifting the *bisj* while they grunted an indescribable sound that can only be written as "Uh!" This is the sound most often heard during Asmat rituals. It is a sound that comes up from somewhere within the rib cage and comes out through the throat, a guttural that the men utter in unison, resounding throughout the whole body.

The pole was suddenly on the shoulders of eight men. All the others were dancing, knocking knees together, flapping hands and elbows, jumping up and down. Each man danced alone, never looking at his neighbor, aware only of himself, as though no one else was in the room. More often than not, they danced themselves up to the very edge of trance. Everyone was perspiring profusely, so much so that the water streaming down their faces and backs streaked the paint on their bodies. None of the Asmat men wore a shirt.

The drums were beating; the men were shouting, "Uh! Uh! Uh!" Together with the yelping, these two different sounds were unique and seemed to shake the walls, shake the glass cases, shake the windows. A procession formed automatically. We began moving slowly, the public dancing together with the Asmat. Everyone was caught up in this celebration, this commemoration of the deaths of five men. The staid hallowed halls of the museum had never seen or heard anything like it and probably never would again.

Slowly, we all moved through the rooms of displays: through the halls of Africa, the halls of totem polls from the Northwest Coast, the halls of stuffed animals. We were being led by Yuven Biakai of the village of Jamasj, head of the Asmat Museum of Culture and Progress in Agats. Yuven shouted out in Asmat a history of his own life and of the lives of the great warriors of his family, who had long since moved on to the Land of the Dead, their deaths long since avenged. All those spirits were moving with us through the museum, for they could surely see, smell, and hear the hullabaloo of the procession. We all were sweating. We continued dancing through the halls, moving more and more slowly until we came to a staircase, went down, turned right, and proceeded through more halls, finally ending at the entrance to the auditorium. We entered with continuing drumming, with yelping, grunting, high-pitched shouts so normal in New Guinea but somehow even more sensational in the museum. The drumming echoed all through those halls.

Yuven, who had been at the head of the procession, led the great crowd into the lecture hall. He jumped onto the stage and screamed out war cries: "Ai! Ai! Ai!" The other Asmat followed him onto the stage, dancing and yelping. The public, too, was in that great frenzy of flapping elbows and hands. At the same time, they were rushing into the theater to find a seat. The auditorium was full within seconds. The atmosphere was thrilling enough to have given everyone there goose bumps.

Everyone was part of the event. When the drumming stopped and all was calm for a moment, the pole was held vertically while an aide from the mayor's office gave a short speech and accepted the *bisj* as a gift from the people of Asmat to those of New York. Yuven rushed to the edge of the stage and started yelping and dancing once again; he then called out the names of his own family dead, those who had been great warriors in their time. He might have been a great headman himself, a leader of raids on villages. It all looked and sounded like the real thing. Yuven leaped and turned and wiggled and did not seem at all like the young man with whom I worked in Agats, who was head of the Asmat museum. The sweetness, the gentleness, the serenity that had been part of his persona were not there then. He leaped from the stage to the floor and continued his gyrations. Suddenly, there was a great "Uh!" and it was all over.

The following day, the Asmat flew to Chicago and the Field Museum.

10

Tateh, Ich vil der Fregen
de fier Kashas

Father Trenkenschuh came to me in Asmat one October morning and said, "How would you like to do an Orthodox seder for us next Easter?" The Last Supper, of course, was actually a seder. I thought it over for no more than a few seconds and answered, "Sure! I'd love to."

Preparing a proper seder in the swamps of New Guinea is no easy matter. I sat down immediately and wrote a letter to my sister-in-law Anne in Great Neck and told her of the request. She must have been surprised at the idea, to say the least. New Guinea? People in New Guinea want to have a seder? There cannot have been many such requests from that part of the world. It didn't faze her in the least. She suddenly found herself as interested in the project as I was. She wrote back to say that she had already begun preparing the package and hoped to get it off within the next two weeks.

I had asked for three or four boxes of matzoh, a jar of horseradish, a bunch of yarmulkes, and a number of Haggadahs that contained the entire service. I would improvise the rest of the necessary ingredients. Obviously, I would not be able to teach anyone the four questions in Hebrew unless the Haggadahs arrived long before Easter. But I did know by heart the words of several songs, including *adir-hu*, and proceeded to transliterate them into the Roman alphabet, wrote them out, and listed a schedule of rehearsals. I chose Father Virgil Petermeier and Brother Clarence Neuner because of their ability to sing in tune. As an option, there was Bishop Alphonse Sowada, who could not carry a tune but was willing to try. He wanted to be part of the singing group.

Trenk, as he liked to be called, knew that I would be amenable to the idea of holding a seder, expecting me to be amused at the mixing of Roman Catholic ritual with a bit of Judaism and vice versa. He also carefully considered an event that had taken place some months earlier when he had invited me to the small chapel in the Catholic mission in Agats, to celebrate the anniversary of his taking final vows in the Crosier order. The other Crosier fathers had come in from their various parishes scattered throughout Asmat to praise him. During Mass, I was, as usual, asked to take part in the ritual of the Circle of Brotherhood and Peace. I had done this before. I was not interested in being converted, nor were my missionary friends interested in converting me. I went as a sign of friendship. I went to commune with myself and to glean that intangible quality of devotion and purity that emanated from them and from the elegant chapel itself. I felt free there, not praying in any traditional sense, but free for my spirit to go wherever it willed itself. My friends had never thought I might pollute their rituals, as some other group might have thought; they accepted me and all my idiosyncrasies.

Trenk led Mass in the chapel. I was in the middle of the semicircle in front of him, in front of the altar. After all seventeen of us had embraced one another, Mass continued and Trenk offered the wine and wafer. I stepped back, as was my wont, not wanting to intrude on High Mass or push myself forward in any way. Trenk came closer, and I stepped back a bit farther. He held out the wafer and said, "Go on, Tobias. Take it. It's the same as the matzoh at the Passover seder." He had a sly look about him. I accepted the wafer and put it in my mouth. It dissolved, my shoulders hunched up in fear. I heard the crash of thunder and saw flashes of lightning. Was that my father turning over in his grave?

How strange and beautiful memory is! When Virgil, one of the young Catholic missionaries, chanted in Latin at his own Mass he always evoked the synagogue for me. And this recalled the records I'd had of Jan Peerce and Moishe Oysher singing in Yiddish and Hebrew. Even in later years, I'd listen to Peerce singing "Bluebird of Happiness" on the radio, corny and sentimental, but it affected me deeply. So I was pleased and excited when Trenk asked me to prepare a seder and Anne was enthusiastic.

Anne was as good as her word, for she posted a package that arrived in March. Some of the matzoh had broken along the way, but the package itself was intact. Everything I had asked for was there. I handed out the

Haggadahs, so everyone had a chance to read the ceremony long before the seder was to take place.

Problems arose. What on earth to do about the *charoset*, which represents the mortar needed by the Israelites to make bricks? It so happened that the girls at the school knew of a *kom* tree on which the fruit was ripe. *Kom* is the size of a crabapple and is marvelously crispy, like a good Granny Smith. The girls gathered the fruit and peeled them. I chopped them with canned walnuts and mixed in altar wine, since no kosher wine was available. The altar wine was sweet, just right for the table but not sweet enough for the *charoset*. *Kom* is very sour. I added a lot of sugar. I swear that my father could not have told the difference between the *kom* and the traditional apple.

For parsley, I substituted *kon*, a wild green leaf we used to make salad. The bishop had radioed one of the Catholic missions in Papua New Guinea, which sent two turkeys. I cut out the thigh of one of them and cleaned it to use as the shank bone. Not Orthodox perhaps, but it did not disturb my sense of rightness for the occasion.

For weeks, Clarence and Virgil and I rehearsed our songs. Not only *adir-hu*, but other songs in Hebrew as well. Virgil often brought along his guitar, which I frowned on. He was as determined to use it as I was not to have it as accompaniment. It didn't sound right. After several tries, Virgil himself decided against it because he could not tune it to blend in with the songs. The three of us sounded pretty good, I must admit. Sometimes, the bishop joined us. We made an interesting quartet.

As kids, we were thrilled by not only the songs, but also various parts of the ceremony. The reciting of the ten plagues was one of them, for it meant dipping one's littlest finger into the glass of wine with each plague mentioned: blood, dip; frogs, dip; lice, dip; and so on through wild beasts, livestock pestilence, boils, hail, locusts, darkness, and, finally, the smiting of the firstborn. Between plagues, we surreptitiously licked our finger after each dipping. In my early memories of seders, we were allowed to drink the wine, giving us all a good taste for its sweetness. It wasn't until much later in my life that I was able to enjoy dry wines.

The Haggadahs were in both Hebrew and English. They gave some explanations for the rituals. The *charoset* attracted the most attention, partly because it was delicious and partly because it represented the mortar with which the bricks were made during the building of the pyramids in Egypt. The bitter herbs (the horseradish) brought tears and recalled the suffering the Jews had gone through during their years of slavery.

At the Asmat seder, there were about twenty of us at table. We all worked together to set up the meal. As presiding patriarch, I brought my own pillows on which to lean. Linens were used for the matzoh covers.

Wine, of course, was altar wine, which we drank from glass tumblers. After my initial blessing of the wine, sung in Hebrew, Virgil, as youngest, read out the four questions. We then went through the service in English from beginning to end, starting at my left and going around, one by one, reading at least one paragraph. We dipped our littlest finger in the wine when we came to the plagues and sucked on it. Sometimes the reading was solemn; sometimes it was exhilarating. Everyone seemed to follow every word. Our quartet sang wonderfully well, even if I say so myself. We'd had enough practice for the bishop, Virgil, and Clarence to know most of the Hebrew words of the songs by heart. The sisters in the convent could hear our singing and sent word that we were to perform these very songs for them. "Come to dinner tomorrow," was the message.

Now, I wonder what my father would have thought about all this, my leading a Passover service for a bunch of goyim in New Guinea, several of whom were dark-skinned. He was not an ideal human being when it came to race relations and had always rooted for Jewish boxers and wrestlers, although when there were no Jews in the ring, he invariably favored blacks.

In Asmat, there were many occasions when I recalled my father. The seder, of course, brought up so many memories that I had difficulty following them, difficulty sorting out what was real. Like the Asmat who ordered a shield to be carved and later so identified with it that he came to feel himself the carver as well as the owner, I invented stories about my very early life, and then came to believe the truth of my inventions. Was my father really as bad as my memory of him insists? Was my mother as gentle and loving and kind and innocent as my recollection? My cousin Ruth answers no to both questions. I cannot remember a time when my father ever talked to me or to either of my brothers; I cannot remember a time when he smiled at any of us, even at our bar mitzvahs. Nor can I remember a time when my mother shouted at us or hit us. She has to have been one of the sweetest human beings who ever lived; she died at the age of thirty-eight, when I was eighteen. My father has to have been one of the nastiest; he lived until his sixtieth year.

Ruth, the daughter of my mother's best friend, Aunt Yetty, and two or three years older than my older brother, insists that my father was generous and kind and was always helpful to those in trouble. She also says that my mother started many of the arguments that took place between them.

Just look at the family photo I've had on my wall for many years. Just look at my mother standing behind Bernie, my younger brother, who sits on a round table or stool, holding (I think) a checker in his hands; I am to his left, and Moe, my other brother, is to his right. My father and my mother's brother Harry flank her. The three children are wearing velvet Buster Brown outfits and sport Buster Brown haircuts. Moe and I are in shorts to the knees, white stockings, and high button shoes. Bernie is wearing what appears to be a dress. He is slightly chubby and has a charming smile. He may have been a year old, which means that I was four and Moe, six.

Looking at the family together, with my father in a suit jacket, vest, and tie, and my Uncle Harry similarly dressed, we appear to be affluent. My mother stands smiling, elegant and beautiful, in a light-colored dress and a long necklace. Her hair fits loosely around her face and is tied in a bun at the nape of the neck. When the photo was taken, we had already moved to Brooklyn from Avenue B, on the Lower East Side of Manhattan. We had a grocery store. Perhaps the year is 1926. We weren't quite so prosperous in the 1930s.

Now, just look at my mother's face. Isn't she beautiful? How could she have been anything but loving and gentle? Now, look at my father, with his cruel eyes and sensuous mouth. Is it any wonder I hated him? And Uncle Harry, doesn't his face express that tenderness that is so obvious in my mother's face?

It is a studio photograph, browned, faded, crumbling. Is the truth of my memory fading, crumbling like the photo? I have never examined the photo carefully, but now I look at it and think of Ruth's words. Is she right?

Think! Didn't we have good times at the weddings and bar mitzvahs and all the other occasions when the family got together? Didn't we watch with pleasure when the poker players assembled in the apartment in back of the store, sat at the big round kitchen table on Sunday nights, and put out their coins and dollar bills, and weren't we thrilled to be allowed to watch until they went home? Weren't we excited, breathless, when asked to run out to the candy store to buy a new deck of cards, receiving a five-cent tip when we came back?

If my father appeared callous and hard-hearted at times, he was always cheerful at the Passover seder. When he beat us—well, maybe not a real beating, more like a wallop or two that knocked us across the kitchen—he seemed to be unaware that we kids thought of him as cruel. We did not understand his moods and never thought his hitting us to be justified. The most important source of his anger was the shelving in the store. It needed constant attention. Empty spaces meant that we should have brought up cases of canned goods from the basement and filled them in before he noticed. Maybe he was hardened by his own father, who had always said, "My father used to beat me; therefore, I am going to beat you." Maybe there is something valid in that. Maybe he was forcing discipline on us, a discipline for which I am grateful. I believe now and have always believed in control and self-restraint; I am up at six o'clock every morning, read the *New York Times* at breakfast, and am at the typewriter by seven.

118

Perhaps he was simply a stern man. It isn't easy to think back sixty or sixty-five of my own years and remember exactly what he was like then. Still, I cannot reconcile what Ruth says about my mother with the way she acted in front of us. I think that my mother and my father never talked to each other, except to discuss the store itself or to mention briefly that he was going to the market to buy eggs. I have no idea what provoked their arguments. My father has been dead for well over thirty-five years, and I still have difficulty understanding who he was. He was generous to his friends, I don't doubt that. He lent them money that they never returned. When he died, a group of his friends owed him what added up to $25,000. We never saw any of it. My sister-in-law Anne, who had married my younger brother, Bernie, got along well with him. She insisted that he move into her house when he was ill and kept him there until it was obvious he needed hospital attention. He was almost lavish in his gifts to his grandchildren. I think she loved him.

If I think back into my conscious mind, let alone try to reach into my subconscious, wasn't my father always laughing when he was with his cronies? Weren't we laughing, too? Didn't we have wonderful Passover seders, the memories of which flood back to me now. Where have I been hiding them? Had I pushed it all back into my subconscious and refused to recognize the better side of his nature? At the seder, he was always seated in a plush chair made plusher by four or five pillows; traditionally, he must be in a reclining position. The bronze candelabrum that my mother had brought from Poland was highly polished; the candles were lit; the *afikomen,* a square of matzoh to be used ritually, and two other pieces of matzoh were slipped into the satin matzoh cover, which was gorgeously embroidered. Children always kept their eyes on the *afikomen,* for the middle one of the three pieces of matzoh is to be stolen and hidden, not to be given up until a prize is offered. The seder, in fact, may not be finished until that last piece of matzoh is found and eaten.

We watched and helped my mother arrange the table with linen tablecloth and napkins, put glasses in place for the wine for all of us, set on one side the bowl with water for washing our hands, and, in the center of the table, put the plate with all the ritual seder elements: a roasted egg, a shank bone, bitter herbs, parsley, and *charoset,* each recalling an aspect of the story of Moses and how he led the Jews out of Egypt.

Passover was a joyous occasion, and we all had a good time. It was our best time together. We all followed the Haggadah as it recounted the story of the Jews' enslavement in Egypt, release after the ten plagues had devastated Pharaoh and his people, and eventual journey across the Sinai Desert to the land of Canaan, led by the prophet Moses.

We read every line of every page of the book. My father read aloud while we mumbled along as best we could in Hebrew. After the blessing of the wine and the washing of hands, the four questions were asked by the youngest member capable of reading Hebrew. The three of us had our turns as the years went by.

We started the questions in Yiddish: *Tateh, ich vil der fregen de fier kashes.* Father, I want to ask the four questions.

Why is this night different from all others? Why on this night do we eat matzoh, why do we eat only bitter herbs, why do we dip the herbs twice, and why do we sit and eat around the table in a reclining position?

It is all still in my head. I will never get rid of it: *Ma nish-tanu ha-lai-lo hazeh mi-kol haley-los.* Why is this night different from all others? The celebration of the Jews' escape from bondage in Egypt, the parting of the Red Sea, the Jews' subsequent trials in the desert, Moses' receiving the Ten Commandments on Mount Sinai, and the eventual sight of the land of milk and honey is an occasion for rejoicing. Therefore, everything on this night is different from all other nights. It is intended to remind us of that astonishing journey out of slavery.

The ritual reading, led by my father, went on until the Haggadah indicated that it was time to eat. We started with chicken soup and dumplings, went on to salad, and then to chicken, potatoes, vegetables. We usually ended with canned fruit and various cookies and cakes made especially for Passover. The reading of the Haggadah continued after supper until we came to the best part of all, the singing of Passover songs. I have no singing voice; that is, Western music always finds me off key. But I can chant and sing in the minor key of Hebrew and Yiddish songs. The songs became part of me, and I often sang them to myself (and still do) at odd moments: riding in a car, traveling on the subway, walking through the park:

> Adir-hu, adir-hu
> Yivneh vey so b'korov
> Eyl b'ney, Eyl b'ney
> B'ney veys-cho be'korov
>
> God is mighty!
> May He soon rebuild His Temple
> Speedily, speedily.
> In our days, soon.

There were other songs, too, all zestful, each with a catchy tune I couldn't resist.

My father had a really splendid singing voice. He could have been a cantor. I never found out whether he, like me, was unable to sing Western music, since I heard him sing only in the synagogue and at home during Passover.

Tateh, ich vil der Fregen de fier Kashas

I see now that there are some positive things to say about my father. I
have to delve deeply for them, but he comes back to me, floating in space,
a smile on his face. The more I think about him, the clearer his image becomes and the more I have to accept some truth in Ruth's version of what
he was like. Didn't he smile at us more often than I want to believe? Even
so, his spirit frightens me, as though I have not resolved the spiritual element of our relationship, just as in Asmat I would have had to resolve it by
avenging his death. He would then have gone happily to the Land of the
Dead, and I would have been able to live in peace.

If I begin to think about him more kindly now, I suppose that one day
I will remember him with affection.

11

The Priest and the Pagans

Father Toon van de Wouw was flushed with anger when he talked to Father Mannheim about me and my book *Wild Man*. He was getting angrier and angrier, building himself up toward the edge of madness. He seemed to be enjoying his own wrath. His body shook; perspiration poured from his forehead, some of it gathering in droplets at his upper lip. Patches of dampness blackened further his black cassock at the armpits. His trembling hands held out my book: "Here! Here! Take it! Read it! You will soon enough see what I am talking about. It is rotten, and I won't have anyone like that here.

"Had I known about him, I would not have allowed him to stay with me or anywhere in my parish. No, sir! I won't have it, and God won't have it, believe me!"

I had not been present at this scene, so this talk comes second-hand. Father Mannheim described it to me vividly, and I have heard him repeat the story more than once.

Father Mannheim took the book, flipped through its pages, and said, "I want to read it very much, now that you have told me what it is about. And I will be pleased to pass it on to all the others." There was a list of a dozen or so missionaries, Dutch and American alike, waiting to read it.

"You watch out, Father," said van de Wouw. "He is going to corrupt everyone. All the boys and all the men! I know his type, and I don't want him here. I don't want that kind of evil in my villages. There is no such thing as sex of any kind between men here, and he is not going to start it!

"Just remember," he went on, "that I stamped all that out when I was with the Marind-Anim twenty years ago. Do you know what they were doing? Have you any idea how they were defiling themselves? Do you know what abominations they were committing? They were using sperm. Yes, sperm. They were using it on everything, rubbing that filth on bows and arrows and spears, saying that it made their spears go straight into the hearts of the enemy.

"I could vomit just thinking about it. They mixed it with their own blood and with lime to make glue. They used the glue to seal the lizard skins onto the top of their drums. Ugh!

"That was nothing, of course, compared to what went on between the men and the boys. That was when they were still initiating nine-year-old boys into sodomy. Apprenticing them to their uncles, learning about sodomy and warfare and how to plant their gardens. And then, then, the friends and in-laws of the uncles also sodomized the boys, one after another, six or seven of them in the men's house. Maybe more. Who knows?

"They told me that the sperm was necessary to the health of the boys, to make them grow into great warriors. Without the sperm inside their bodies, they would not approach manhood, they would never become powerful warriors. It is the work of the Devil. And I stopped it completely. It took a while, but I assure you that it is all gone."

Father Mannheim waited while Father van de Wouw gathered himself together for further revelations. "Here in Asmat," he went on, "they used to have wife exchange—*papisj,* they call it. Of course, they had an excuse, claiming that the flow of semen was necessary to keep the cosmos in balance. I quickly put a stop to that, too. All it really was, was another excuse for an orgy. They know it is against God, just as they know that sex between men is against God."

Father van de Wouw, unlike the other Caucasian missionaries in Asmat, was not a Crosier. He was a missionary of the Sacred Heart and was rather inclined to look down on other Roman Catholic orders. He was a relatively narrow-minded man on this subject and was insistent that only missionaries of his own order had the direct line to God. He was slender and handsome, his body taut, reflexes sharp and alert. He had a long hooked nose that might have been deemed Semitic had his lips been more than a tight thin line. "No!" he insisted. "There never was any homosexuality in Asmat, and it is going to stay that way, believe me."

Father Mannheim had related the conversation to me soon after he learned that I would be traveling with Father van de Wouw to Ladakh, in

India. He wanted to make sure that I knew what I was getting into, that I would be with a man who despised me and who despised all homosexuals.

I never hid my sexual proclivities during conversations with the missionaries. I did, however, restrain myself when it came to personal relationships with Asmat men. I liked to spend time in van de Wouw's villages because they were in an area rarely visited by outsiders at that time.

During my early days in Asmat, I stayed with Father van de Wouw three or four times and learned a great deal from him. His knowledge of the people, although limited in some ways, was remarkable. There was much about him, in fact, that was admirable, including his knowledge of the Asmat language. I was discreet in my behavior, not for my own sake but for that of the people themselves. Even matters of a nonsexual nature sometimes were difficult to discuss with him.

One day, an elaborate memorial celebration in honor of recently dead relatives was taking place in the village of Japtambor, close to van de Wouw's home in Basim. Both of us were invited to attend. Although the feast itself had begun several months earlier, the final formalities were to begin the following day. The feast was an exhausting and exhilarating time, an occasion into which we both entered enthusiastically—in the singing, the dancing, and the eating—with almost the same excitement as the villagers themselves.

On the morning after the celebration, church services were held in the roughly built schoolhouse that doubled as a church. No one in the village had yet been baptized, so the service was short, with no Mass being said. Almost immediately after van de Wouw began, he announced that the adults could leave, but the children were to remain for instruction in catechism. I went to the men's house to continue my questions about the carvings and the ritual works that had been made for this particular ceremony. Some minutes passed before I became aware that a group of fourteen men was standing around me. Suddenly, they were lifting me horizontally and grunting in unison, "Uh! Uh! Uh!" They carried me to one end of the structure, turned and carried me to the other end, and then carried me back to the center, where they stopped, still grunting "Uh! Uh! Uh!" I was still being held horizontally.

The men's house was full. The grunting continued while the man at my right shoulder bent down as though to kiss me, but moved instead to suck my nose. He sucked my chin, and then sucked my earlobes. He sucked my fingers one by one, sucked my nipples, opened my shorts, sucked my penis, and finally sucked each of my ten toes.

When the first man had passed my nipples, the man next to him bent and began sucking my nose, then my chin and earlobes, making the same rounds as the man before him. The third bent and then the fourth, and in this way, each of the fourteen men sucked all the extensions of my body. It thrilled me, and I was as though in a dream, floating as the men carried me, my ears and head filled with the sounds that reverberated through my body. The men took up my penis and sucked it, and I was thinking to myself, Why am I not erect? It was all without reality, without sensuality, mysterious, otherworldly. No one seemed to expect me to have an erection, nor did the men handle me in a way that might have aroused me. When they put me down, there was a great hullabaloo of shouts. I did not know the meaning of the ceremony, but it obviously had to do with adoption into the village.

Then, no sooner was I breathing normally when I heard sounds coming from outside the men's house. I heard "Uh! Uh! Uh!" I looked out. Father van de Wouw was being carried from the church to the men's house for the same ritual sucking. The number of men around him made it impossible for me to see what was going on, but from the bobbing heads, it had to be that the men were sucking his nose, his chin, and his fingers. Then it was obvious from his shouts that he would not allow them to lift his cassock. "Stop! Stop!" he yelled. "Put me down! Put me down!" Later he said to me that these practices were barbaric, and he would put an end to them.

Still later, I learned that the ceremony was performed primarily for the men to absorb my strength by ingesting the fluids of my body, part of a ritual adoption. In this way, I would be a permanent member of Japtambor, my juices already inside the bodies of other men. It excited me no end that some part of myself, if nothing more than sweat, would be spreading within the fourteen men who had absorbed my secretions. In the same way, the men ate the flesh of their enemies, taking into themselves additional power and fierceness.

The men did not neglect me during those hours of rituals when van de Wouw slept peacefully in the teacher's house. The men's house, by then, reeked of armpits, and I breathed in the air as though it were sweet and fresh. They took my hands and rubbed them on their chests, and then they rubbed them on my own chest so that I took on their sweat, the essence of their strength.

I felt completely at home in Japtambor and did not hesitate to recommend the village to a German filmmaker by the name of Friederich who came into the area. The year probably was 1979. He had had an introduction to the bishop, and the bishop introduced him to me, asking that I take him to a village in the south. Quite naturally, I chose Japtambor for the film's location, since it remained one of the few places where some aspects of traditional life continued. Father van de Wouw also agreed to take part, to make sure that all commentary and scenes were culturally correct.

During the three weeks we were together, Friederich treated me and van de Wouw like servants, even slaves. Later, neither of us would accept money for our respective roles because Friederich seemed interested only in the violent side of Asmat life. However, in lieu of financial payment, he invited us to join him on a five-week journey to Ladakh the following summer, all expenses paid.

In Asmat, Friederich showed himself to be egocentric, with everything revolving only around himself. All thoughts of possible personal problems with him, however, faded when it came to the actual moment of flying to Ladakh. Going there was too exciting a prospect. Both van de Wouw and I expected to be able to cope with his oddities, as well as with each other's. By then, there was an unspoken truce between us.

A chauffeur-driven Mercedes met us individually at the Frankfurt airport, and we spent two full days at Friederich's house. He was wonderfully generous and outfitted us with parkas, boots, and the other usual paraphernalia for trekking in high mountains. A small incident in Frankfurt should have put me on guard. Friederich brought out three small rugs that he had bought in Ladakh some years earlier. "Marvelous!" I said. I looked at them carefully, commenting on the tightness of the weave, the golden colors, and the intricate design. "Did you know," I asked in all innocence, "that all Muslim carpets have a mistake woven into them?"

"What do you mean by that? A mistake in *my* carpet? It is not possible!"

"Oh, yes," I said, wanting to show off my knowledge. "Every carpet has one."

He was upset that I had dared question his eye. I simply wanted to point out that all Muslim carpets have a small fault woven into them on purpose. Only Allah can achieve perfection.

We flew off to Moscow via Aeroflot, probably the most rattletrap airline on earth at that time. Everything on the plane seemed to be loose and shaky.

In Moscow, we changed to an equally unpleasant craft and equally unpleasant stewardesses. We disembarked in New Delhi, switched to Air India, and continued to Kashmir, a marvelous flight. Friederich had bribed all the visible Soviet officials, thus enabling us to board without payment for excess baggage for the camera equipment, the heavy luggage, the tents, the sleeping bags, and a trunk full of boots.

There were seven of us all together, five mountain climbers in their twenties and thirties, plus van de Wouw and myself, both in our mid-fifties at the time. In Srinagar, we were taken to the most luxurious houseboat on Lake Dal, had a splendid lunch, and began preparing for the sights after a brief rest.

It was already four o'clock in the afternoon when Friederich announced that we were going to a factory to look at carpets. We were herded into three horse-drawn carts and were kept at the factory for five hours. "Now," Friederich said, "we are going to the Oberoi Palace Hotel, where I lived for six weeks seven years ago, when I was making a film there. It is one of the great hotels of the world. There is nothing to see in Srinagar."

After coffee, we returned to the houseboat for supper.

"Everyone up at four o'clock tomorrow morning! No more sightseeing here," Friederich yelled at bedtime. "Set your alarms, if you want good seats in the bus!"

Van de Wouw and I, by this time, were treating each other as though we were good friends. The difficulties between us did not surface. We discussed our lack of freedom from Friedrich, but not much more. There seemed no anger on the priest's part.

It was still dark the next morning when we climbed into a bus that clattered and bumped through the eastern Hindu Kush, passing through the lushness of the Vale of Kashmir into the high arid deserts of Ladakh. The road twisted and turned above the Indus, the great river lined with trees and fields of wheat. That evening, we arrived at a small hotel in Kargil and accepted the rooms assigned to us by Friederich. Van de Wouw and I were put together. He was obviously nervous about sleeping in a room with me. He was polite but distant. He never discussed his true thoughts or feelings. The room we shared was cell-like, with two narrow beds and a small, low table. We had had separate rooms on the houseboat. I was nervous and thought I would not sleep, but slept very well.

Van de Wouw said nothing that night. He blew out the oil lamp on the table between the beds and began to undress in the dark. In the morning, I was up first and went out to wash, giving him time to dress alone. The water was fiercely cold.

"Damn!" I said when I came back. "Friederich is getting to be too much. He is out there now opening all the doors and screaming for everyone to get up. I do not know how much longer I can put up with his odd behavior. Aside from the fact that I don't give a damn about climbing mountains. I'm interested in the people and the monasteries and the religion. Climbing mountains is not my thing."

Van de Wouw agreed: "Let us figure a way out."

For two whole days, we stood in the back of a truck, shaking and bouncing, while the vehicle jolted and creaked, cracked and tilted, farted and groaned, climbed to 17,000 feet, twisted itself on twisting, rocky roads, and, finally, arrived at Padam in Zanskar on the second evening, just as it was getting dark. We had spent the previous night on a great plain in icy temperatures, in sleeping bags covered with several blankets. We slept inside a huge tent, while outside winds blew at fifty miles an hour.

127

We all looked ghostly getting down from the truck, covered with the fine white powder churned up from the roadway, all except Friederich, who had been sitting in the relative comfort of the truck's cab.

By then, van de Wouw and I had decided on our story: we were too old for a walking trip so high in the mountains. Not only were we sick of Friederich, but spending two weeks trekking through snow-covered mountains without seeing people or monasteries seemed wasteful. I had been reading extensively and intensely on Hindu and Buddhist religions since my early teens and felt that looking only at mountains in Tibet would devastate me. I had no interest in proving my strength through climbing rugged peaks, beautiful as they were.

The plan had been to start the trek the following morning. We asked Friederich for five minutes of his time. Van de Wouw began: "Friederich, we have a confession to make, and we are afraid you won't like it. Please be patient with us. We have now been around these mountains four days, and we both find it exhausting. The altitude is too much for us. We are afraid we will hold you up and delay your schedule. We see now that we are too old and should not have come."

"No, no," Friederich said. "No need for apologies. In New Guinea, I thought you both were strong when I saw you walking through the jungle. But now I see how difficult it will be at your time of life. After all, we Germans are a strong people, and we are used to cold climates and the difficulties of climbing mountains." There was a good deal of satisfaction in his voice. Both van de Wouw and I might have had problems on the journey, but neither of us doubted that we could make it.

"We hope you aren't too disappointed," I added. "We can take a truck back to Kargil and make our way slowly to Leh and meet you there."

"Perfect! I will give you the money. It will be an easy trip from Kargil, and if you have trouble, if you get too tired, just stop and rest wherever you are. You will have plenty of time before we get there." Friederich was suddenly solicitous, as though we were decrepit old men, which is what we wanted him to think. There was a spirit of conspiracy between van de Wouw and me.

That night, I read aloud for the first time from *The Asian Journal of Thomas Merton*. Merton had not been in Ladakh on his last journey in 1968 when he died so tragically through a faulty electrical connection in a hotel in Bangkok. He had studied Buddhism and Tantra and had been at the court of the Dalai Lama for some time, traveling mostly in northern India, where he had written of his fascination with Eastern religions. He saw no reason for Buddhism not to act as an extension of Catholicism, believing that he could take it into his heart without allowing it to affect his Catholic tenets. In the appendix of the journal, a glossary and notes explained in detail a lot of what we were seeing and what we were about to see.

As we moved from village to village, from monastery to monastery, I read aloud more and more often, in buses, in places in which we ate, and in the small and large rooms in which we slept on stone floors. At first, van de Wouw would not listen to anything that might include sexual connotations.

"Pollution," I read, "is the spilling of the seed without union, without fertilization or discipline, without 'return' to the summit of consciousness. A mere spilling out of passion with no realization. 'The end of passion is the cause of sorrow, the precipitation of the [human consciousness].'"*

This passage disgusted van de Wouw, even though it is difficult to understand. It seemed to be against physical and mental masturbation. But as we read on, he began listening and questioning everything. We read passages over and over again, both from Merton's pages and from the appendices. Even the word "Buddha" needed an explanation:

Literally, an awakened or enlightened being, from the Sanskrit root "bodhati"—he awakes and understands. The name usually refers to the historic Buddha; that is, Gautama Siddhartha (563–483 B.C.), born near Kapilavastu in India, a member of the Sakya clan, and hence called also Sakyamuni, the Sakya sage. . . . It is important to stress that Gautama was only one of many Buddhas who have existed before him and are destined to come after him.[†]

Oddly, I was able to explain a great deal that was not in the book through my own knowledge. We talked, too, of Judaism and Christianity.

"But how is it that you, a Jew, should know these things?" he asked.

"What does being a Jew have to do with anything? Or being a Catholic or Muslim for that matter? I told you that I started reading of other religions right after my mother died. Buddhism had always interested me, and I could not imagine myself climbing these mountains and looking only at the landscape, when there is so much else to see and know."

We spent days in monasteries, sometimes with lamas who understood enough English to talk to us in depth. I, for one, believed their stories of reincarnation and listened to the men talking about the *Tibetan Book of the Dead*. It took us both a long time to begin to understand the differences between the Gelugpa (Yellow Hats) and the Nyingmapa (Red Hats), the two sects of Buddhism practiced in Tibet. This was partly because the

*Thomas Merton, *The Asian Journal of Thomas Merton* (New York: New Directions, 1975), 90.
[†]Merton, *Asian Journal*, 370.

lamas themselves could not verbalize it properly, and partly because Merton quotes a friend who says, "There is no difference."

It was through our talks, as well as through our reading, that it was possible to see that van de Wouw, for the moment, was opening up, beginning to expand his vision of religion and of life. He, too, seemed to believe in the reincarnation of the lamas who spoke freely to us and in such detail of their past lives. We sat listening to experiences that presumably had taken place hundreds of years ago, and we both fell under the spell of the men recounting tales of former lives. We never questioned the truth of what they were saying. The look on their faces and their manner of speech told us that they could not be lying; they believed and had an aura about them of other centuries. They often seemed enveloped in a halo of spirituality.

Van de Wouw and I shared a room everywhere we went, sometimes sleeping next to each other on carpeted stone floors. He appeared to have lost his fear of me, no longer apprehensive that I might attack him. Since we stayed in monasteries where Tantric Buddhism was practiced, we talked of Tantra, too, and of its ritual use of orgasm as a stop along the way to enlightenment. It seemed miraculous to me that we could speak of such matters openly. In my eyes, the use of sperm for magical purposes, retaining it and thereby using its power, was no different from what had been happening among the people of his parish in Asmat.

After several days of talk, van de Wouw appeared to accept the fact that sexual activity could be necessary to early stages in the training of lamas, that the act itself brought forth a dynamism that gave great strength to the spirit. He said he could understand that the orgasm might even become the ultimate form of spirituality for those deeply involved in Tantra. At least he was able to discuss it, whether or not he understood or felt its sensibility. As lamas go to the higher stages of their spiritual development and the sexual act continues, the orgasm itself is held back. Adepts are brought to the point of climax but no further, so that they might contain its power, for it is this power that leads the adept closer to Nirvana. Van de Wouw agreed that this might be possible, but he could not or would not connect it with the way of life in his own villages. He would not allow me to bring up the subject, insisting that there was no comparison between his wild and savage people and the highly civilized Tibetans.

Shortly before leaving New York for Ladakh, I had been to see a practicing Buddhist. He had lived for two years at the court of the Dalai Lama in Dharamsala, in northwestern India. There were many followers of Tantra in the Dalai Lama's retinue, and it was to that group that my new friend had attached himself. He was homosexual and, when I met him, was completely open about it, although I never would have suspected his orientation through his appearance or gestures or voice or attitudes.

Some months after his training began, he told me, he declared himself to his Superior. "There is nothing wrong with homosexuality or in practicing homosexual acts," the Superior said. "You must remember, however, that such acts should be limited to your first years here. You will learn that everything must be directed toward perfect balance, the *yin* and the *yang* equalizing each other, the male and the female balancing each other. Only through sexual acts between men and women is it possible to go on to the next stage of spirituality. You must pass beyond homosexual relations before you can begin to absorb your own semen into yourself. By retaining your semen, you will eventually transform yourself; you will move, however slowly, along the road toward becoming a bodhisattva, perhaps eventually achieving Nirvana."

To my knowledge, my friend did not reach the point of retaining his orgasms, but he was remarkably self-contained and had an inner peace that enabled him to remain calm, at least on the surface, no matter what the circumstances. I recently learned that he is now living in a remote valley in the Catskills, continuing his prayers and meditation.

Van de Wouw and I talked of the sexual act in impersonal terms, although I suspect that he had never performed any sexual act, including masturbation. However, he must have had wet dreams in his youth. We certainly could not talk of people we knew. He simply closed up when I approached the subject of the people of his parish. It is one thing to discuss sexual matters in an alien land about alien people, but quite another to discuss people we knew personally. He was horrified at the thought of the young men he knew imbibing semen to give them the strength of great warriors.

I wanted to stay on in one of the monasteries, to learn, to become involved. The square faces of the men, with their high, prominent cheekbones and their shaven heads, seemed to glow with purity and strength, and eroticism, too. They chanted, they meditated, they laughed. Their lives, from the outside, looked gracious and elegant and mysterious among the paraphernalia of their ceremonies.

With van de Wouw in such close attendance on me, it was not possible to become more friendly with the monks. I needed to be able to sleep anywhere, to enter into their religious atmosphere with complete freedom.

Van de Wouw was trying, I think, to reevaluate some of his beliefs. Perhaps, given the choice, he might have stayed on for some time longer, studying the religion a bit more in depth. Merton, although a Trappist who had obtained permission from his superiors to break his order's vow of silence, had concentrated on understanding some Eastern beliefs and had remained a deeply religious man, a true Catholic.

By the time we parted, van de Wouw appeared to like and to trust me. He acted as though he had reversed his earlier judgment. I could not be sure of his true thoughts, but after we rejoined Friederich and the others in Leh, I sometimes heard him praise me and my "vast" knowledge of the religions and the way of life in Ladakh. On the flight back to Frankfurt, he said, "You know, Tobias, I have spoken against you many times. I disapproved and still disapprove of your way of life. But I can see now that not all other ways are necessarily wrong. On this journey, I had to accept the fact that your knowledge goes deeper and wider than mine when it comes to religious life, and I admire you for that. And I must admit that I could never have made this trip without you."

Months later, I heard through Father Mannheim that van de Wouw had spoken to some of those in Holland to whom he had complained about me and had told them of his new attitude. He seemed to be another person. Soon after van de Wouw returned to Asmat, however, I heard again from Father Mannheim that he had reverted to his former self, complaining about homosexual acts and condemning the use of semen in any way but for reproduction. It saddened me that he could not keep to his new insights, but had fallen back into the pattern that had molded him as a child, as a postulate, as a young priest. Perhaps he was frightened of his own sexuality. Perhaps he realized that the men of Asmat had been lying to him for years, a fact he could not absorb.

12

Line 6 Juliet

An exploration company, ANSA, looking for oil in the foothills of the Jayawijaya Mountains above Asmat, invited me to its camp on the Brazza River through its manager, Roberto. I was there primarily to collect artifacts for the museum in Agats. There was, however, an implicit understanding that I would write something positive about the company.

"Just imagine an oil spill in Asmat!" he said when we first met in Agats. "It doesn't matter what the company says about its policy of taking precautions. It is inevitable that there will be a spill." The Asmat are hunters and gatherers who obtain all their food from the forest and from its rivers and streams.

"Just think about this great swamp and all the sago trees. Just think of even the smallest of spills, the oil seeping out and covering the surface of the water, the tide coming in, the oil spreading farther and farther into the jungle, the tide going out, the oil settling into this vast peat bog." Roberto vowed to quit his job and return to Australia.

"Sago trees are fragile and are easily destroyed," he went on. "What will happen to the people and the forest then? Everything will die. It will mean the death of the environment and the death of Asmat itself."

The Brazza camp was comfortable and pleasant. A series of mosquito-netted huts had been put up for the Europeans. They were collapsible and were easily put together. When properly used, they kept the mosquitoes at bay. Three immense tarpaulins, pegged and poled, covered the cots of the

Indonesians. Jerry-built huts had been pieced together for the kitchens, and solid housing had been constructed for the latest in seismographic and radio equipment. The food was excellent. Western-style for the Westerners—steaks and chops, fresh vegetables and fresh fruit flown in daily from Darwin, about 800 miles south on the Australian coast. Sometimes, I preferred eating the Indonesian fried rice with the workers.

There were no women in any of the camps. The Australians and Americans were given a week's leave for R&R in Singapore or Bangkok every third week, travel and hotel expenses paid. I never asked, never learned, what the Indonesians did to relieve their sexual frustrations and could only surmise that their appetites could be contained more easily than the appetites of the Caucasians or could be pleasantly satisfied among themselves within the camp in the dead of night.

The camp on the Brazza was easily reached by one of the two company helicopters, although their use was restricted to the Aussies and Americans, except when moving an entire camp to a site a mile farther ahead. The helicopters brought in the Europeans and the equipment, sometimes carrying huge Caterpillar tractors and bulldozers piecemeal to level the forest, while a boat carried the Indonesians. Senggo, farther downstream, had a small airstrip and a small hospital run by Protestant missionaries. The strip was large enough for the helicopters to land, flying almost directly north, from Darwin.

I first went up the Brazza in January 1976. The only travelers into the area had been two or three Europeans and some Indonesian crocodile hunters. Those who were looking for local people made very limited contact or none at all.

The base camp at Senggo was considerably larger than the camp on the Brazza and had permanent wooden structures. Everyone was friendly, generous, and eager to talk to me, an outsider who was there only to make contact with the local people, not to work with the esoteric equipment, about which I knew nothing. I watched with open mouth while each of the Australians drank a case of beer (twenty-four cans) every night, between 5:00 P.M. and 11:00 P.M., and did not have a constant stream of piss gushing from his body. It intrigued me that so many hours could pass without their having to relieve themselves, unlike the American helicopter pilots, whose capacity was as limited as mine.

I was in the Brazza camp when the information was relayed via radio that four Indonesian policemen were missing, presumed to have been killed by the people of the upper Brazza. Two bodies were later seen floating downstream, one with long arrows protruding from its chest. The witness to these floating corpses said that he had seen one body clearly enough to identify it as one of the men from Palembang in Sumatra. The dead man had been shooting domesticated pigs belonging to the Koroway, an act that would have demanded violence in return. Koroway pigs are easily identified by a thread looped through the top of their ears and by the fact that they do not run off at the approach of humans. I wrote in my journal:

25 February 1976, the Brazza. I was told today that Baldo had flown into Senggo from Singapore and would be returning to his camp on Friday. If he agrees, I will go with him. We have spoken only briefly. He says there is a Koroway house close to his encampment.

Baldo is a Bulgarian who escaped from Europe to Australia just before the end of World War II. He is in charge of twenty-five men who are cutting a foot track, called lines, through the forest.

It rained heavily here and in the mountains this morning, raising the level of the river at least twenty feet since my morning bath. Tree trunks with roots entangled, bunched up and formed massive mounds of islands, many with egrets resting atop branches or on the lookout for fish. The air is cool.

27 February, Line 6 Juliet. Line 6 Juliet are the coordinates of our location on the company map. The map, in its entirety, comprises an area of various tribal peoples, including the Koroway, the Kombai, and the people of the Brazza. Each has its own language, incomprehensible to the other. The Kombai and the people of the Brazza carve war shields, the Koroway trade for theirs or steal them in raids.

I arrived just an hour ago at this jungle camp by helicopter, literally the only way to get here. Bad weather delayed the journey. Baldo is out on the line with the men. Curt, one of two American pilots, veterans of the Vietnam War, brought me in. He had flown along the south edge of the Jayawijaya Mountains, passing over the Kolff, the Modera, and the Eilanden Rivers. The flight was breathtaking, swirling in cloud one minute, sweeping up the side of a mountain the next. Line 6 Juliet is in the crotch of the Eilanden and Weehuizen Rivers. We noted several houses from the helicopter, each one high on stilts, looking deserted, as if it had not been used since the arrival of foreigners a year ago. Most of the roofs had caved in. The eaves of one of the low houses reached the ground. The house was a long one in which several families would have lived.

From the air, we could see great stands of sago within the forest. Many of the trees had already flowered and are therefore no longer edible. The swoosh and pull of the helicopter is like a ride on a roller coaster. The cabin is a plastic bubble, allowing the pilot and two passengers (more are possible) to see up, down, to the right and left but not to the rear. The chopper tilts and sways, blurring vision. It is joyous and scary at the same time. We seem to fly directly into the mountains and suddenly rise on an elevator shaft of currents.

Line 6 Juliet

The helicopter offers views of sharply inclined mountains covered with forest, with vertical cliffs down which waterfalls rush. Yellow-crested cockatoos fly up with raucous cries, hornbills flap their great wings, flying foxes, awakened from sleep, squeal out their displeasure; stands of sago palm are close by small gardens of taro, cassava and banana trees.

Line 6 Juliet is a platform of logs about 25 feet by 35 feet, on which the helicopter lands, where the cooking is done and where our bed rolls and mosquito nets have been placed by Josef, our cook and general helper. A stove and a small refrigerator represent our kitchen. "Josef is the best cook on the lines," says Baldo. Plenty of food is stuffed into the fridge. The chopper arrives every day with fresh meat, vegetables and fruit and at times with mail. Josep had been trained at a Catholic mission on the island of Flores, where he was born. He is dark-skinned and has frizzy hair.

There is a house near us, perhaps Koroway, perhaps Kombai. From the helicopter, no people are visible. The next day, I climbed the rickety ladder. The fireplace shows ashes that have been dead for days. Two pigs come into our camp to investigate smells from old garbage. I follow their trail to the gardens of bananas and a vegetable that, in its husk, looks like a thin ear of corn, *tebu tellur* in Indonesian, *finam* in Asmat. The path on which I walk goes from garden to garden but to no house that I can see. The trail to the house is cleverly hidden. I wander through the forest alone.

I walk on and feel the stinging pleasure of the immense forest around me. I walk where there is no sound but dripping water and the crunch and snap of twigs and branches as I clumsily step along the narrow trail, made by animals and humans. There are occasional calls, whistles, shrieks, howls, all to warn against my approach. It is a momentous time, for as always when I am within the forest, I draw energy from everything growing around me.

Dusk is upon us, Josef is working on the Butterfly pressure lamp. He fills the bowl with fuel, fills the cup with alcohol. He lights the alcohol, pumps the lamp and adjusts the glow of the light. Night's descent comes quickly, a cliché about jungle contrasts, but within the brilliance of the lamp it is as if daytime remains. Outside its perimeter there is nothing but blackness. The brightness of the moon seems to make shadows appear darker than they are. The sounds of insects and animals rise in pitch and volume.

Lines are cut parallel to one another; that is, the men hack out a rough trail just wide enough to walk along for a kilometer or so. Several trails are cut, each by a small team. Another is cut vertically to the first, forming a grid. Other men go through and, at cross points, dig holes in which they plant one-pound sticks of dynamite. At the proper signals, the dynamite is blown up. Sound waves penetrate the earth down to 5,000 feet. Readings are taken seismographically, recorded on paper 10" by 24", interpreted in Jakarta. At the moment three groups of men are cutting lines in different areas.

Line 6 Juliet

We are in dense jungle. Often, I stand still simply to admire the forest itself. The only opening to the sky is above our helipad. A pig and two piglets approach our camp to forage. Frogs, invisible when still, pop up and leap along the earth. They are nothing but blotches of black, gray and white, indistinguishable from the rotting mass within which they live. The smell is of mold. There are endless loopings of vines. The trees reach up as high as two hundred feet, their roots twisting and curling, the banyans dripping air roots, the strangler figs rising high to strangle their host trees. Sometimes the forest seems nothing more than a mass of tree ferns. There is a great variety of epiphytes but no orchids seem to bloom at the moment. A sense of freedom comes over me, erotic thoughts compel me to shiver.

28 February, Line 6 Juliet. Baldo, my host, is a handsome man with curly hair verging on blond. His skin is pale, as if he had never been in the sun. Here, just below the Equator, he is in the forest, always dense enough to keep out the sun except along the rivers. We are awaiting the chopper with the nurse who will give Baldo the last of his penicillin shots. He came down with the clap in Bangkok, his preferred site for R&R.

"I am ashamed," he said. "I never had a sexual disease before and feel sick about it. In camp, everyone jokes about the clap and about sex itself. I am too ashamed to speak the way they do. Curt, the pilot, talked as if his language had nothing but 'fuck' in it. 'I fucked sixteen fucking times over the fucking weekend. Those fucking girls are fucking hot.' Or, I hear, 'I went the whole fucking night without ever losing my fucking hard-on. My cock never went down, not for a minute. Those girls are hot, man.' There is no chance for that in my country. We have whores, yes, but not like this and they are examined every week by a real doctor." I did my best to convince him that there was nothing shameful about what he had done, only that he had failed to use a condom.

Baldo is a rough, delightful sort, with a thick, intriguing accent. Late last night, we went to the stream to bathe, as we do every night. The moon, shining through the leaves of the forest, lit our way. We did not need our flashlights but took them anyway. The silence was broken by the laughter of Indonesians coming back from the stream, proceeded by the light beams of their lamps. They wore sarongs and carried towels over their shoulders. They held their guns and rifles in front of them, terrified of surprise attack.

"They are all trigger-happy," commented Baldo.

The stream is cold and clear, nine or ten inches deep. It rushes over rocks and gurgles as it dips into small pools. I sit and wash with soap. I lay back on the stones smoothed and rounded by hundreds of years of water flowing over them. I look up into the sky. We are part of the jungle, part of the Milky Way. Baldo stands and washes himself, soaping his penis and testicles again and again, producing an erection.

"I am afraid of disease," he says. "I must clean every part of me properly," he says. He cups and holds his testicles and again soaps his penis.

"I will never have a whore again. It isn't worth going through this fear and anguish."

This morning before eight, we went walking along the line. The richness of the forest enveloped us. Twenty minutes later, we came upon a trail made by the Koroway. We turned into it and passed two gardens before coming to a clearing with two deserted houses. The larger house was about eighteen feet above the ground, built on scaffolding of slender logs. The ladder was a single notched log four inches in diameter, typical of the Kombai. The floor must have been 30 feet by 15 feet. Inside were four fireplaces, the ashes cold, scattered. Bone and animal remains were stuck into the crosspieces of the peaked roof or were hung in bunches. Skulls and whole skeletons were part of the ritual and spiritual decor on walls, as well. There were no human bones that I noticed.

Wherever I put my foot and weight, the branches and flooring cracked and crashed. A death might have forced the family to abandon their home, or, it might have been the intrusion of outsiders.

We continued along the trail and came to another house. Again, there were bundles of bones hanging from beams. A rack had been built under the flooring, a place for storage of food, tools, other items of daily use.

I went out on the trail again as soon as Baldo went back to the lines. I suddenly ran into two trotting Koroway men who looked 16 or 17. They were terrified of me, their bodies shaking with fear. They were carrying heavy loads of green bananas from their foreheads and had been so bent over they could not see anything in front of them. Both shivered and would not put their loads down. Both had an earring in the right earlobe—a loop of cassowary quill on which were threaded bits of cuscus fur and the beaks of small parrots. The hair of their foreheads had been interwoven with what looked like thin slivers of reed. They wore dog tooth necklaces, rhinoceros horn beetle proboscises curled up from the tips of their noses. Wooden pins were inserted around their nostrils.

They tried to run away. I moved to entice them to stay with gifts of knives and tobacco but they did not look at what I held out and accepted nothing. They would not look into my face. They backed off and looked so frightened that I let them go. I wanted to follow but they disappeared into the forest too quickly.

I wandered that trail for another two hours and saw stands of sago, wild jackfruit, gardens of bananas, of taro. The Koroway were surely watching me but I never saw or heard any movement.

Later that night, with the buzz of insects around the mosquito net and the calls of night animals coming from the forest, I thought of that encounter with the mysterious Koroway. I had truly frightened them, appearing so suddenly out of nowhere. I wanted to make contact, give them gifts, smoke one of their pipes together with the men, see the house in which they lived, take photos, trade for whatever they might agree to trade, for what I might find interesting for the museum. In my eagerness, in my excitement, I failed to think about them and what their reaction might be. I had thought it would be a simple matter of gifts but they were too frightened. Perhaps the stories they had heard of outsiders has so terrified them that nothing could alleviate their fear. Perhaps they looked at me as a vengeful spirit who could destroy them with nothing more than a look in the eye.

29 February, the Brazza Camp. Baldo and I went up in the helicopter this morning to get the lay of the land. No more than two kilometers from the pad, a new house appeared with smoke seeping through the roof. The smoke disappeared as soon as the chopper was heard.

The immense chain of the Jayawijaya Mountains rose up spectacularly in front of us as soon as we climbed above the trees. The day was clear for the moment, with no more than a few puffs of cloud to hide the snow-covered peaks. Curt, again our pilot, took us close into the foothills. We saw a house, then a man running through a short clearing into the forest. He stopped and crouched behind a tree while we hovered above him. There was a dog on the porch. There were other houses, as well, with smoke still rising from their roofs. Back on the ground, we started out again on foot to look for those elusive houses. We walked for hours, partly on the line, mostly on jungle trails but saw no one.

The Koroway live in small clusters of two or three houses, making a hamlet population of 18 or 20. They do not live on the banks of rivers and all paths to their houses are well hidden.

Back at the encampment, an announcement on the radio said that Baldo's leave to Australia had come through and the helicopter would pick him up in an hour. His departure saddened me. I asked for his address but he said he would never write.

2 March, Brazza. The day started out with a call from Mike, head of a team of Indonesians working Line 71. The men had come upon an active settlement of houses and had stripped it of stone axes, spears, necklaces, bows and arrows, everything they could find. The Koroway had been surprised by men cutting the lines and had run off into the jungle, leaving all belongings behind. Mike called for steel axes, machetes, and other goods to replace what had been stolen. The man on the radio yelled into the microphone that the men must put everything back. The stolen artifacts, however, had already been hidden away and no one in the camp admitted to having seen any.

6 March, Brazza. Went alone in the outboard up the Brazza River, reached the mouth of the Assamur River, a tributary of the Brazza, and turned into it. I was then traveling a river on which none but local people had ever been known to travel. The noise of the engine disturbed and frightened the bird and animal life; the human life, as well. It wasn't long before I saw several banked canoes and a man half-hidden behind a tree. I called to him, "*Ndein! Ndein!* Come! Do not be afraid!" The man was obviously alarmed. He peered at me, apprehensive, curious, tremulous, bold, wanting closer contact but not knowing what my reaction might be. This man had obviously heard of outsiders, people with white skin. Suddenly, he came out and revealed the whole of himself, a courageous move. He was naked but for grasses tied into his hair and the body decorations that included a leaf that seemed to cover only the head of his penis. The body of the penis, in fact, was hidden, pushed back into the scrotum, the foreskin pulled forward and tied with a fresh leaf. His modesty did not include covering his testicles, a tight ball of them which was left bare. I asked, in a language of gestures, to see his house. He came into the outboard and accepted the plug of tobacco I offered, enough for several dozen cigarettes. He smelled the tobacco and smiled. Other men had also been there all the time, invisible, part of the forest. The color of their skin and their ability to be perfectly still without sending out vibrations that outsiders could sense, allowed them to blend in with the environment. One of the men had voluptuous breasts. I thought at first that he was a woman. All wore long thorns through their nostrils, in addition to the sticks of various lengths, like toothpicks. The men were attracted by the sight of the tobacco and came down to the boat.

A man, whose name turned out to be Sher, sat on the bottom of the aluminum boat. He bent over to smell the metal, a substance he had never seen before. He licked it with his tongue, knocked it with his knuckles.

The men jumped up and down, laughed, yelped, climbed into their canoes. We all waved and shouted. Within a few minutes, we were in a shortcut that took us back to the Brazza. We tied up near the mouth of the Assamur. There did not seem to be any opening into the forest but no sooner were we ashore, when we were walking on a narrow trail that led to huge felled trees, three or four feet in diameter. The trees had been cut down with stone axes, directed so they would more or less fall end to end. Several men, standing on a platform surrounding the tree, seven or eight feet above the ground, chopped away at the trunk. Later, I had a chance to see the men in action, hacking away, one after another, a method more efficient than I would have imagined. End to end, the logs formed a road through the jungle. Slippery for me, but not for those who lived there, who ran along logs as if on a racetrack. The men were aware of everything around them. They saw my need for help before I recognized it myself. They held onto my elbows and allowed me to hold onto their shoulders from the rear, the easier way for me to walk without slipping.

Several hundred feet into the forest, a long house rose like a structure built from an Erector set that used wooden elements instead of metal. flimsy-looking poles and one tree trunk held up the house. Slats of sago bark formed the walls, roofing was of sago leaf or pandanus. A group of men mottled with light and shadow, stood beneath the house. They waved and shouted as if they had been expecting me. Dogs howled and rushed up one of the ladders. They stopped at the porch and whined at me. The men kicked at the dogs with their bare feet. The women screamed and ran off.

Line 6 Juliet

The rungs of the ladder were spread widely apart. Children managed climbing more easily than I did. The rungs were thin and looked too weak to hold my weight. I grabbed the sides of the ladder, afraid that one of them might break but they were as hard as ironwood. Inside, were fireplaces and sleeping mats of a single spathe of a sago leaf. The floor was uneven; I had to watch where I stepped, afraid I would trip and fall through. Bark cloth was used as blankets.

Fire was brought to life from embers and sago was baked. I looked around and saw various items for which I later traded: decorated smoking pipes, Jew's harps of bamboo, net bags of orchid fiber, nose and ear ornaments.

I asked about shields and two youngsters were sent out. The Asmat word for shield is *jamasj*, almost exactly the same as the word here, *jemesj*. An hour later, two shields were brought in. I caught my breath at their beauty. Suddenly, the whole world came together. They made an uncommonly deep impression on me for they emanated an extraordinary power. The symbols, their shapes and colors of red, white and black, were spaced out almost haphazardly. Yet they had the magical quality of the shields downstream among the coastal Asmat. I recognized only one of the motifs, the flying fox, a design repeated five times, not spaced out in any traditional Western way, with one half of the shield reflecting the other half, but with a force of design that gave them the balance and beauty of true art.

The world calls these men and their artifacts primitive, but what I saw there was of rare beauty—intensely energetic designs that verged on cabalistic motifs and a powerful, fascinating people who deeply understood the world of spirits. They had learned to cope with the violence around them, of warfare, of storms, of the terrors of spirits, of daily life itself. They had taken these facts of life and transmuted them into an art form that reached beyond the boundaries of their own world and affected all those who were receptive to their singularity. They had, in fact, translated their fears into Art, not an easy task.

The men offered food while trading transactions were taking place. I traded an ax, a machete, fishing line and hooks and other valuables for each of the shields. Later, other shields were brought and I bought them all for the museum.

The women returned warily. Fearful that I would put the Evil Eye on their babies, they covered the children's faces with blankets, and covered their own eyes with their hands. I gave them fishhooks and nylon line, and gave everyone tobacco. I spent several days and nights there, enjoying their hospitality.

Soon, all of life will change. What will the people look like in clothing? Their carriage will change, the way they move will change, the way they stand or walk, all will be so different, the people will be unrecognizable. The same men and women, without facial decorations, with tattered shorts or dresses and tattered shirts, will give an appearance of someone from another part of the world. I was helping that change, even though I had no clothing with which to trade. I did have metal tools and that would change the whole character of the shields.

Line 6 Juliet

Back at the Brazza camp, everyone was surprised that I had not been killed by the "savages." After that, I kept the borrowed outboard loaded with gifts when I went upstream. It was loaded with artifacts on the return trip.

In a calmer moment, Roberto said, "We are killing them off, one way or another, as if we were shooting them one by one." Every day, Roberto gets more and more depressed as he contemplates the destruction of the forest and the people. He needs his R&R or home leave or a new job.

Farther upstream, still on the Brazza, men screamed out from the bank of the river, yelping, anxious to make contact, anxious to trade. They came down from their tree houses to look at me, to watch the boat pass by, to touch me if possible. They had learned that I could be trusted and that I brought gifts in exchange for artifacts. I had stolen nothing. We visited and traded. The men were calm and delightful, excited by the axes and machetes and other metal that I brought. They did not appear to be nervous, although none had seen a Caucasian before. The women however, ran at the sight of me.

My reputation as peace-maker and interpreter burgeoned, as well as my untested reputation for bravery. I was always naked with the local people so they could see that I had no weapons and was as physically vulnerable as they. The Australians called me a warlock because I talked to the people and always returned from the forest in good health, with my head still attached to my body.

One day, the radio announced that the Koroway had blocked the line leading straight to their tree house, putting up human skulls and bones to magically stop the intrusion of foreigners. As the line neared the house, arrows flew in the direction of the work crew from somewhere in the forest. The workers took their orders literally and cut their lines straight, with no deviation from the shortest distance between two points. Gardens and houses were often in the way; the lines went through willy-nilly. One of the lines on which Mike's men are presently working is scheduled to go right through one of the houses. The house will be destroyed.

It was suggested that I go ahead of the crew to clear the way, to talk to the people and offer them gifts. I told Roberto that the Koroway would not know me and might even kill me. They are different from the people of the Brazza and have had only frenzied contact with the groups around them and no contact with complete outsiders. They do not seem anxious to trade. I am not distinguishable from the others on the line, from the Indonesians of Celebes, of Java and Sumatra, from the Australians and Americans, those who have shown nothing but violence toward the local people. It was too late for me to make friends. Even so, I said I would try to help.

10 March, the Brazza. Tommy, the company spy, arrived yesterday and stopped me from going up in the helicopter. "He is not insured by the company!" he shouted. "You cannot take him up. It is against company policy!" I heard him screaming about me several times. He seems unable to speak in a normal voice.

He was furious when he heard that I had already been in the helicopter several times and railed at me and everyone else about it.

15 March, Senggo. I was sent back downstream, but then I had dinner last night with Sam, manager of the holding company that hired ANSA. We got along well. When he heard of my contact with the people of the Brazza, he asked me to return to Koroway territory as consultant and liaison out on the line.

"Never mind about Tommy. I will take care of him," he said.

Trouble has started out on the lines again. Two days ago, a member of the crew disappeared and was found hours later, hysterical, sitting in mud on the bank of the Brazza. He said he had been captured by the Koroway who live several rivers from where he was found. He said he had been taken to their house but he escaped down the ladder and had run away while they were examining his machete. None of the Australians or Americans believed his story. It was too implausible that he could have escaped. Nor could he have found and followed the hidden trails. He had probably been frightened by someone or something, ran, got confused and couldn't find his way back to the line.

20 March, Brazza. Had an uncomfortable lunch yesterday down in Senggo with Tommy, Sam, Harry, and Roberto. Tommy is as narrow-minded as he is narrow-bodied. Sam is top man in Jakarta, good-hearted and intelligent. Roberto, enclosed within his own thoughts, hardly said a word. Sam said a construction company would be coming over from Papua New Guinea to widen and lengthen the airstrip at Senggo so that DC-3s could land. Drilling will begin in the area of the Brazza within weeks.

Tommy was miffed that his order preventing me from riding in the helicopter was overruled by Sam. At lunch, Tommy suddenly began asking questions, all very pleasant on the surface but with obvious suspicion and anger.

"I am sure you are sending weekly reports to the Rockefeller Foundation about what we are doing here."

"Tommy, what do you mean? I have no connection with the Rockefeller Foundation, only with the JDR 3rd Fund."

"But we know, don't we? We know that they are the same family and we know they work for the CIA."

"I honestly don't know anything about that. My work is only for the museum in Agats. All I am interested in is research on the life of the people here and in collecting artifacts."

"Still, you must be sending in reports on everything that goes on here. I see you writing in that book of yours all the time."

"Of course, I have to write in my journal or I will forget everything I see and hear. I really am here only to collect shields and other material culture and information about the people. I am grateful to ANSA and the Holding Company for their help and hope they understand that there is nothing political in what I put into my journal. You are welcome to read it any time."

Line 6 Juliet

Later, Roberto said that had Sam not been there, he would have punched Tommy in the mouth. He and Harry, an executive of ANSA from Jakarta, had sat there quietly, saying nothing. Tommy was despised and feared by everyone.

Now, at 9 A.M., I am waiting to go out on the line with Mike, to see if anything can be done to calm the Koroway. I listened to a report on the radio of eight men who had been carried out in the chopper after being wounded by arrows. The Koroway were described as a race of giants, monsters, in fact, immensely tall, massive, with boar's teeth curling down like moustaches from their mouths. They were like no other people around, the report said. The two young Koroway I had met on the trail were diminutive, of course.

23 March, Line 103 Bravo. Have been going out for three days and have seen no people. I climbed one of the houses, eighty or ninety feet above the ground. A wind high in the trees made the house sway scarily. The highest house had a simple ladder that divided itself in two about two-thirds of the way up, like a Y, one ladder going to the women's entrance, the other to the men's. It was not an easy climb. The crackling sound of the rungs as I put my weight on them was frightening; the movement of the central tree trunk gave me a feeling of falling and made me dizzy.

When I reached the floor of the house, I could see inside. A human skeleton lay there comparatively small, perhaps a woman or a teen-ager. The bones were intact except for the rib cage, which had collapsed. A curled gourd penis sheath was stuck into one of the walls. The Koroway wore them. Like other houses of the region, there were animal bones, shells and feathers decorating the underside of the roofing.

In the clearing were two small gardens enclosed by a fence, to keep out the pigs. Inside the fencing, bananas and taro grew. Not far away a bird and animal blind had been built on the ground, a simple tepee-like structure of leaves and branches, in which a man with bow and arrows or spears could sit and wait for whatever came to drink at the nearby stream. In one house, I saw sections of bamboo used as water containers, wooden and bone needles, bone scrapers, and a brush of pig bristles. Leeches were attacking the blood of my ankles.

24 March, Line 103 Bravo. Mike and the men were stealing whatever they found in the houses, in spite of protests from the head office. We walked the line, one behind the other, me first, Mike next, then his co-workers. We reached the end, where seven policemen stood with rifles and machine guns at the ready. Just beyond the end of the line, a long rattan vine stretched across the trail and into the jungle on both sides. From the vine hung three human skulls and some spears. The skulls had been cleaned of their flesh. The whiteness of the bone meant the skulls were relatively fresh, for they did not have the patina that colors a skull after continued use as a pillow, as the men use them downstream. I wondered what I was doing there. It was obvious that the Koroway would start shooting their arrows as soon as the workers started cutting into the gardens and there was no way to stop the policemen from pulling the triggers of their rifles. To them, the Koroway were the enemy, the dangerous ones. The skulls and the spears meant, "Do not cross this line! We will kill you if you do!"

The Koroway were surely around us, waiting to see what would happen. They could easily have killed us all. They might have killed me first, as I stood there alone.

Instead, they chose not to reveal themselves.

I called out several times, *"Sini dasan! Sini dasan!* Don't be afraid!" but there was no answer. After a while, I went back to where Mike was waiting. I asked him to keep the men from going on, to keep them from knocking down the house, that I would spend the night there, on the line itself.

The floor of the forest was cleared and a rubber mattress was set on criss-crossed twigs and branches. Mosquito netting was tied up. Axes and machetes and other trade goods were left around as gifts. I hardly slept at all. There were too many noises that might have been anything from squirrels to the Koroway themselves.

I learned the next day that three policemen had also spent the night there, close to me. When it was full daylight, Mike came with a thermos of coffee.

I saw immediately that the gifts had not been taken and the skulls and spears were there as well. We were soon greeted with a shower of arrows that hit no one. Even so, the machine guns blasted out and sprayed the forest in all directions. The silence that remained was deafening.

The seismographic device indicated that there was oil beneath the surface. An entire town was set up at the confluence of the Kolff and Siretsj Rivers with all Western amenities, including electricity twenty-four hours a day. Six months later, fresh water burst forth from the ground instead of oil. The town was removed as quickly as it had been brought in. Nothing physical remained, only the memory of it in the minds of the people.

I feel a strong sense of relief that ANSA has given up, that, for the time being, the forest and its people are safe from destruction. I also know that their destruction is inevitable.

13

Death

For years after my mother's death, I caught glimpses of her in the subway. She was thirty-eight when she died; I was eighteen. She would just be turning a corner, suddenly hidden behind a steel pillar. I searched her out, ran after dark flashes. She haunted my mind and body. She was like a Balinese *leyak,* one of the spirits of humans most often seen in the form of a blue flame that darts from coconut tree to coconut tree, at night. A flash here, another there, disappearing, then reappearing just at the edge of vision. The Balinese, according to Miguel Covarrubias, say that when you are naked and bend down and look back between your legs, you will surely see a *leyak*. Covarrubias defines a *leyak* as "a person who through knowledge of black magic can assume weird shapes to harm others.* Foreigners are not aware of them because they are shy of strangers.

Unlike the calm spirit of my mother, a *leyak* is intent on doing only black magic: making people sick or destroying the crop of rice or spreading disease among the pigs. *Leyaks* are responsible for most of the problems that come to Bali. Doing harm was not my mother's way. She was sweet and gentle and loving, all things a child expects in a mother.

The Asmat do not yet understand the process by which a woman becomes pregnant and believe that it happens only through contact with frogs. Frogs are everywhere in the swamp. A frog will hop along the floor

*Miguel Covarrubias, *The Island of Bali* (New York: Knopf, 1983), 325.

of the forest looking for a woman with whom it will bear a child. It sees a woman and watches her carefully, examines her countenance, watches what she does. It sees that she is an attractive woman, but that she is a poor parent who beats her children. "No," the frog says, "I do not want her to be the mother of my child. She is too mean." The frog looks again and sees a woman sitting in the forest doing nothing. The frog looks closer and realizes that she, too, is not what he is searching for. She is lazy and does not take home enough sago for the whole family. Finally, he comes to one who seems to have no faults. The frog suddenly jumps up and smacks the woman right in the chest, thereby impregnating her.

My mother needed nothing more than her own heart to know how to be a good parent. She would surely have laughed at the frog story. She was as unlike Asmat women as she could possibly be and needed only to allow the seed planted in her by my father to germinate and then await her child's birth. Yet I remember that we talked once about a story in the Torah. I said, "I cannot believe that Sarah was able to have a baby when she was so old." My mother answered, "It was God who allowed it," giving the story a validity it would not otherwise have had. She had the kind of faith that accepted everything. "Life is in God's hands," she would say.

My mother would never have done evil in any sense, never have purposely caused trouble. When we had no money, she cut her long hair and sold it. She nurtured me and my brothers through the usual childhood illnesses and never panicked or broke down. Once, in our kitchen, when my younger brother tripped while running and fell onto a pair of scissors he was holding in his hand, she seemed to be there instantly, lifting him up. The scissors jabbed into his throat, leaving a bloody hole that Dr. Kopp later sewed up. Nor did she panic when she carried me to Dr. Kopp after I was hit in the eye with a fragment of a cherry bomb, on a Fourth of July. I was delivering orders from our grocery store, and was just turning the corner of Third Avenue into Senator Street, when I heard an explosion and saw a group of boys scattering in all directions. I felt a flicker of pain at the edge of my right eye, but I continued delivering the orders and thought nothing more of it. On the way back to the store, the wife of Nick the shoemaker called out, "Come here! What is wrong with your eye?!" She took me inside to a mirror, and I gasped at the blood on my cheek. Tears welled up in my eyes. My mother said nothing, simply picked me up and, passing right by my father, who was behind the counter, took me straight to the doctor. "I told you so!" my father yelled at me. "I told you never to touch fireworks!" my father called. "Now look at what's happened!" The fragment had hit the very corner of my eye, but had done no permanent damage. A bandage covered it for weeks, forcing my sight into a new aspect of vision, one without perspective. It was a curious and frightening time, with my whole eye covered. I was a spectacle at school and shied away from contact with other students.

The Balinese have good spirits as well as destructive ones, of course, assuming that they pay proper attention to the rites that appease the dead. Offerings of food, of flowers, and of prayers at the Temple of the Dead are necessary, in addition to the eventual cremation of the body and the accompanying ceremonies that release the soul so that it might go on to other worlds. Cremation is by no means a sad occasion; it is a time for celebration, a joyous event, for it liberates the soul of the dead from attachments on earth, preparing it for reincarnation.

Like my mother, I am an implicit believer in the spirit world.

I am, in my own way, surrounded by a spiritual atmosphere: after all, I am named after each of my skulls from Asmat, as well as having been named at birth after a relative who is said to have lived to the age of 108. So take care, for I may well have inherited a gift for the supernatural from my mother. Do not forget that I have within me the combined strengths of all those for whom I have been named in Asmat, whose skulls now brighten one of my bookcases. Of course, this includes the head of Sembet, father of Ndocemen, who gave me the name Sembet, thereby instilling within me the spirit of a man who had taken five heads in battle, aside from the powerful name of my venerable relative. It must never be forgotten that names can kill. The Asmat believe that if you know the real name of a man or woman and you want to harm him or her, you can take that name into the jungle, shout it out, and thereby kill that person. In former times, when someone reached one of the several crucial stages of human life, such as initiation or marriage or first menstrual period, a new name was bestowed to record the event. Today, of course, with Christian missionaries around and villages under government control, the birth of a child is immediately recorded and names are given to the baby.

My mother understood and lived in a world of spirits, just as the Balinese do, just as my Asmat friends do and just as many other peoples of the world do, although the spirits might have different names and different attitudes. My mother seemed to me to be a medium through whom contacts with the dead and even with the living could be made. She rarely told us tales about life in Poland. When she did, they were mysterious, full of allusions to spirits and to the Lord God in Heaven, with whom she spoke directly. My father was equally reluctant to talk of his homeland. It was only recently that I learned that my father's parents had owned the local lumber mill before World War I and had been relatively affluent. This was not the image that came to mind about my grandparents on my father's side, based on snippets of conversation among relatives. In my thoughts, they had to have been poverty-stricken, barely able to pay the passage in steerage of

Death

five dollars from Gdańsk to New York. I learned this not from either of my parents, but from a relative who visited us in the rooms in the back of the store once or twice a year.

My mother and father never talked to each other, as far as my memory tells me. True, he would say, "I'm going to the market now to buy eggs." Or he would say, "You watch out for the Poilisha, or she will steal every-thing in the store." Nor did he ever speak to us directly, only in some tan-gential way, as though he were afraid to look into our eyes, as though he were looking at some *ndamup* or *djuwus*. He would sit at the kitchen table, reading the *Jewish Daily Forward*, rocking back and forth in the tra-ditional style of reading from the Torah or reciting daily prayers. At almost set intervals, he burst forth with incantations that commented on the sto-ries he was reading, stories that might have been meant only for himself, but, in fact, were meant for us to understand.

My father's dictum, "God will strike you dead!" was shouted out whenever he saw one of us committing the cardinal sin of turning on the light during the twenty-four hours of the Sabbath. My mother never made such pronouncements, never berated us. Instead, she filled us with com-passion and faith in the most subtle of ways. Her few stories riveted us; rather, they riveted me, for I was the recipient of most of her confidences and her trust. Or it appeared so to me, for I felt closer to her than I imag-ined my brothers did. Perhaps, in my self-centeredness, I missed the deep bond between them. Perhaps jealousy blocked out their images. Or I might have attached myself to her more often and more tightly than did the oth-ers, feeling her sympathy, her nearness, the warmth of her body, needing the nourishment she offered. It gave me the courage to face my own weak-ness and the lack of masculinity that seemed to be part of my being. It is not that I missed masculinity in myself, for I would rather have played a recording of Beethoven than play a game of baseball or whatever was de-manded from students in high-school gym. Now that I have tested myself through journeys into the wilderness among a sometimes violent people, I feel that I have no fear of death itself, only of pain and suffering. I won't know the answer to that until the time comes. I continue to encourage my-self to take risks. I have no problem with whatever the word "masculinity" means. Of course, listening to Beethoven has no connection with being queer, but that is what my schoolmates seemed to think. Listening to clas-sical music was, according to them, equal to being a fairy. "Roll Out the Barrel" was the top tune of the day.

My mother would surely have been terrified of *leyaks* and all other spirits of the night and the forest. She had never indicated any degree of fear, including fear of her own death. I remember vividly the way she looked those last weeks of living on Third Avenue in Brooklyn, propped

149

up in the big double bed, stricken not only with cancer of the womb, but with aphasia that stopped her from speaking in an articulate way. She would look at me as though with yearning, and I would repeat the sounds that came out of her mouth in an attempt to understand what she wanted. She looked so sad and forlorn, as though she were in a foreign land, abandoned by everything and everyone she knew.

My mother had one close friend, a woman she loved, whom we called Aunt Yetty, although blood ties were distant. She came from the same small town in Poland from which my mother and father had come. They had been friends there and had migrated to New York at just about the same time. I think we lived in the same building on the Lower East Side before we moved to Brooklyn, or maybe it was only on the same block.

My mother had other good friends, as well, but it was Aunt Yetty who visited us most often, even after we were settled in Brooklyn. She used to bake the most extravagant pastries and bring them to us. On each of our bar mitzvahs, she arrived bearing a fourteen-layer cake with white icing that she had carried on the subway in the huge cartons in which boxes of laundry detergent used to be packed and shipped. She and my mother used to sit in straight chairs, fingers interlaced in their laps, and rock their memories into existence. Aunt Yetty's laughter was almost continuous when she and my mother were together, but we knew that she had problems with her husband. Somehow, we heard that he was too lazy to work, although Aunt Yetty herself never complained. She later became the matriarch of the family.

I can still conjure up the bright light in her intelligent eyes. She was a spiritual being, for everything about her flowed, as though to illuminate universal love. I never understood that aura around her until years later, after my time in Ladakh, when I remembered her sitting in chairs that enthroned her. In my memory, I gave her the air of a bodhisattva. She never sat cross-legged in lotus position, but there was a solidity about the upper part of her body, as well as a restfulness to her being, that always put me in mind of lamas in meditation. If her generous ability to laugh seemed to contradict this spiritual quality, I have only to think of those lamas I met in the Himalayas who joked constantly with one anther, yet had an essence of sanctity about them.

Sometimes, when there were no customers in the store and my father was at the market buying eggs or in the kitchen playing pinochle, and my brothers were in our backyard playing catch or fooling around on the horizontal bar, my mother and I would talk and sip from glasses of tea at the kitchen table. When she reminisced about the past, her eyes and face were often streaked with tears dripping over her high, almost Oriental cheekbones. These times were too rare to learn much about the family's history. However, there were occasional stories that remain embedded within me.

"My mother's sister was ill, one winter," she began, as though continuing a tale that she had previously begun. I had never heard her speak of this relative before. "My aunt was so ill," my mother went on, "that nothing could save her. All the family crowded around the bed, moaning, wailing, waiting for her to die. Everyone loved her, she was so good and so beautiful. No one knew what the illness was. She just got sick one day and was at death's door the next. My mother loved her more than the others of the family, maybe even more than her own six children. She opened the door and went out into the cold, taking only her shawl and babushka against the wind. She had a look of pain on her face that radiated beauty, as well as her suffering. She trudged through the snow into the potato fields. She knelt and looked up into the heavens. 'Please, God,' she cried out. 'Please don't take her. Don't take my sister away. She is so kind and so gentle. She never harmed anyone and now she is dying.' My mother wept and moaned and wailed. She beat her chest with her fist and cried out again and again. 'Please, God, do not take her. Take me, instead. Take me!' God did not send a crack of thunder and lightning into the sky, but He had surely listened and heard her anguished cry. He took her unto Himself the next day. We found her in the snow in the morning, barely breathing, her whole body shaking. With her last bit of strength, she told us how she had spoken to God and that He had listened. Her sister immediately took a turn for the better and lived on for another six years."

I always asked for stories about living in Poland, but few were forthcoming. When two of my mother's brothers came to New York in the mid-1930s, they, too, neglected the past and spoke only of the present and future. My mother's older brother died nine months after her own death, but of colon cancer. My own brothers died of it, as well. I, too, had surgery on my colon twenty-five years ago, a resection, obviously a success, although inactive polyps remain. They don't bother me, and I don't bother them.

The memory of my mother always evokes two images: one of her, the other of my friend Dorle. They looked very much alike and fit into the same physical pattern. Both were thin, both about the same height, five feet, perhaps a bit less. Both had the same reddish-brown hair and prominent, hooked noses that hark back to the Semites before the Diaspora, I suppose, for Dorle is Sephardic, while my mother was Ashkenazic. Dorle, as of December 1997, is ninety-seven years old, a year younger than my mother would have been, had she lived. I gave a dinner party on Dorle's birthday. She drank her usual gin and tonic, followed by wine with dinner. She smoked most of a pack of cigarettes. Age has not affected her intellectual capacity. Ninety-seven years old or not, she is fascinating and continues to be remarkably bright and witty, still incisive in her comments on opera, literature, and music.

At the State Theater with a good friend, Rick, for the ballet, some months ago, Dorle suddenly felt heavy on my arm, as though she had collapsed. I looked down and saw that she could not stand. Her head was bent; her knees were bent. Rick was holding onto her other arm. We carried her to a bench and sat with her. When she began to gag, as if to vomit, I went in search of a doctor, but none was on duty in the theater itself, only backstage. We sat and tried to calm her, hoping that this was not the end. She looked more ancient than ever. Recovering slightly, she took out her wallet, handed it to Rick, fearsome that he would be out of pocket if she died then, and urged him to take the money he had laid out for the tickets. Her wrinkled face was grim, more lined than ever, her hair uncombed. She sat there as though death were rapidly approaching and would soon take her. Within minutes, however, she was fine. Whatever had caused the attack seemed to have passed. "No doctor!" she said, and was adamant about it. "Let's go watch the performance," she said, and we did. Later, we went to the Iridium for dinner, across from the theater, had drinks and wine and good food. Dorle puffed on one cigarette after another, as though nothing had happened. She didn't eat much, but had a small bowl of risotto. I had the rice, as well. From Dorle's nephew's wife, we later learned that she probably had had a very minor stroke, not for the first time. Rick confessed to me that he had been terrified that Dorle would die then and there. He has never seen death. "I hope," I told him, "that I or someone else close to Dorle will be with her when it happens. Much better than dying alone." In the cab, on the way home, she talked about the ballet we had just seen, choreographed by Balanchine to a violin concerto by Stravinsky, and commented favorably on the dancers and the performance in general. She was in excellent spirits.

Dorle is my oldest friend. I've known her for thirty years and more. In the beginning, I was always hesitant to talk to her because of her immense knowledge of singers, musicians, and opera, and simply because of her sharp intelligence. She has always been involved with music and had, together with her late husband, owned a recording company in Italy, Cetra Soria, that produced classical music and opera. Later, the company was sold to Columbia Records. She knew everyone in that world and had been a good friend of Maria Callas and of most of the great and lesser stars of the Metropolitan Opera from the 1930s onward.

Every once in a while, I think of Dorle being in such comparative good health and wonder about the agonies of the two Davids, Jimmy, Michel, Charles, Riccardo, Timothy, the two Kevins, Sam, Steven, Dennis, Raymond, all good friends who died of AIDS early on in their lives, before reaching middle age—except for Maurice, for he died of AIDS at the age of eighty-four, died with his boots off, so to speak.

In Asmat, too, many friends have died, not in warfare, but in accidents like a tree falling or a canoe turning over or even an epidemic of cholera coming suddenly, taking charge of who is to live and who is to die. In particular, I think of David Simni, of Ndocemen, and of Ee, one of the men who worked on the bishop's boat, whose name always pleased me to hear, for Ee means "pee" in Asmat. I do not know whether my good friend Aipit is still alive in Japtambor; or any of the other friends I made during my time there. Even Ben of the village of Sjuru and Natalis of Jamasj were still fine when I saw them last in 1995.

The great age difference between all of them and Dorle is deeply saddening, with Dorle living through almost the whole of the century, while these young men disappear into the earth or are fired into ashes and scattered in beloved places. They are at both ends of the span of life. Do they cancel each other out? Isn't it particularly moving when comparing Dorle with Rick, Dorle's youngest friend, at twenty-nine, and a friend of mine as well? Can you imagine that Rick says he loves me, and I believe him? Can you imagine that he comes into my bed at times, and we perform beguiling rituals? It is heart-breaking to see this young man naked and especially gratifying to feel him inside me. What am I doing with someone so young? Am I drawing his strength into myself? Is he giving me something of his younger days, taking me back into my own younger years? What is he doing, coming so late into my life, so early in his? What does it mean? I have always been almost fifty years older than Rick, and I will always be almost fifty years older. Where was I all those long years of my youth and middle age when I hid inside myself and avoided closeness? Was it simply that, at long last, the spirits in my apartment have come together and egged me on to complete openness, to acquiescence, to recognition that I am somehow worthy of love? Have all four compartments of my life come together now, to make me whole?

Of course, I know that Rick loves me even now, just as I know that Douglas still loves me. I do not dare to compare the two men; they are like two sides of a coin, ready to be tossed in the air or spun like a dreidel, offering new paths of exploration. I think about Douglas often, only partly because he was in New York recently, on a six-week visit. The Arts Council of New Zealand had given him a grant to look at dance in New York and in parts of Europe.

Those months and years between Douglas's departure and Rick's arrival on the scene, when I was finally mature enough to begin to understand who I was, when Douglas had exhilarated me and Rick had pushed me farther into freedom, weren't all those early years after my time in Asmat? Wasn't Douglas after that time? Wasn't all that after I had absorbed all I could from the Asmat? Wasn't it the Asmat—Aipit in particular—who first allowed me to develop into a man, whether or not it was their semen that led the way? If they could suck my body's extensions and absorb the essence of me, doesn't it work the other way around as well? Even though old then, I felt I could only gain through every single act of fellatio or sodomy. What do the Asmat know that I have yet to learn? What further course of study will lead me deeper into their secrets?

In the canoe, the paddle in my hands, movements are akin to chi kung. I am Lifting up the Sky for Health, energizing my body, and Carrying the Moon for Youthfulness, emptying my brain of thought and breathing myself into relaxation. I can envision Rick now, at Glimmerglass, working as assistant to Paul Kellogg. I try to dismiss Douglas's image from my mind when I am with Rick, and vice versa. It doesn't work, but he is content; I am content.

I think about Gabe's suffering from some still-undiagnosed disease at a neural terminal in the back of his neck, a triple fusion of vertebra that ruptured, leaving him in such pain that an operation was necessary. It was not a success. After a year and a half, he is still never without pain. How do you get through years of physical pain without respite? Narcotics help for twenty minutes at a time, no more, not worth the addictive drugs he has been on. For the past ten days, he has been taking something new, a drug used specifically for those with trans-geminal neuralgia that may work for him. It is too early to tell. He is forty-one, but even with his constant agony, he looks to be only in his early thirties. Recently, he registered for a course leading to a degree at Vermont College.

Last week, we sat at table in the Villa Mosconi on Macdougal Street, with me on Gabe's right, his mother, Paula, on his left, and then Martin and Floriano. Looking into his face as he sat next to me was to look at the whole of *Homo sapiens,* to look at unyielding solidity and courage, a face of surpassing beauty, all angles, a squared-off jaw. It is a countenance that appears to be at rest, but in truth is holding up a mountain of vulnerability and uncertainty. Perhaps he, too, is rolling that stone up the mountain, only to have it roll back down again. This man, when well, had spent his life in tranquillity, exuding compassion, sending out no disturbing waves. His past has girded itself up to help him. Is he now continuing to store up *sakti,* the Balinese spiritual, magical energy that counterbalances the dreaded work of the *leyaks?* He remains soft-spoken, more often silent. The look in his eyes goes so deeply into himself and into me, as I look at him, that I begin to feel that I can understand the entire cycle of life, the history of mankind.

Outside the restaurant, he walked as though treading on eggs that he

154

knows will break. Yet he appears to have no anger in him, only a determination to accept his present plight.

Into what corners of this earth, what corners of our body, do Fate and our genes lead us? Age, AIDS, neural disease, heart disease, cancers here and there, life itself—all lead to death. They lead to pain and anguish, physical and mental. They lead, too, to moments of passion, love, sympathy, exhilaration.

I thought of the story of the Westbeth resident who had crawled out onto a terrace to escape the oppressive heat of his apartment. He looked across the myriad low structures, the pots of plants, and the entangled vines to the Cunningham Studio, ablaze with light. It was the hour of darkness before dawn. The air was still; a mood of quietness had settled over the city. No one was visible. A silhouette suddenly appeared, a shadow, a gazelle leaping from one window to another. Within seconds, the mystical figure took the shape of Merce Cunningham himself, at age seventy-five. The leaps were those of his youth, high and elegant, swift and eloquent, his agonized, gnarled toes disappearing from sight and distance and spectral light. The whole of his body was masterfully controlled, exuberant, an expression of life, the measure of a man's passionate need to create and live until his own last moment, no matter the pain of his body and mind.

14

Evocations

Sembet's skull is nestled in one of the bookcases in my apartment among six other human skulls. They are decorated with the feathers of a sulphur-crested cockatoo, with red abrus seeds and gray coix seeds that have been knotted into a net headband that holds the feathers. One of the skulls has a bamboo nosepiece; another has a nosepiece of shell cut into a spiral to imitate the tusks of a wild boar, a head-hunting symbol. Still another is without decoration, but has a hole in the left temple, indicating that it was taken in battle and used in initiation ceremonies. The hole, made with a stone ax, allowed the cooked brains to be poured out.

In Sembet's village of Sjuru, when I walk by, wizened old ladies, their faces creviced with wrinkles, call out: "Sembet-o! Sembet-o!" The added "o" is a sign of affection. They are my mothers, my sisters, my aunts. My presence, my name, recalls the spirit of Sembet, a great warrior who had taken five heads in battle, his name now mine, his power and ferocity now mine. I could take his wife as my own, had I wanted her, for I am truly Sembet himself. His children, too, are mine, and my brothers-in-law, were they still alive, would bring me food: sago, shrimp, pig meat. Only a few years ago, I was given an additional source of power: the bow and arrows of Sembet.

Ndocemen, volatile and violent, had long since adopted me as his son, naming me Sembet for his father, hanging his skull around my neck, not suspended on my back, where lesser men wear theirs, but resting against my chest, proof of my potency. Ndocemen, too, is dead now, his body buried in mud, unlike the corpse of Sembet, which had been wrapped in a mat of pandanus leaves, placed on a platform in front of the men's house, and left there to rot until the skull fell away from the neck bones of its own accord, the skull inherited by Ndocemen and later handed down to me.

In this way, there is continuity between New Guinea and New York, with my body and spirit returning there each year, taking on gifts for my family and always bringing back additional energy and omnipotence. In this way, too, my life is around me in my apartment, madeleines and touchstones, every object on walls, tables, bookcases, all alive, feeding me vitality, serenity, intuition, inspiration for what I write.

Attached to the bookcase in which the skulls sit, and projecting from it, are two old prowheads from the island of Anoes, off the northern coast of Irian Jaya, where the influence of American GIs during World War II can still be heard in the broken English of elderly men and can even be seen in old camouflage jackets and shirts, half rotted away. Above the skulls and prowheads, atop the bookcase, a painted ceramic pot from the Kei Islands, given to me by Sister Dee of the mission in Agats, sits next to an Asmat prowhead carved with three human figures and a black king cockatoo, which leans against a slightly broken Wosera shield from Papua New Guinea.

But it is my walls, my walls, that define me, protect me; rather, it is my war shields hanging there that give me sustenance and life, for the spirits within them not only take me back in time, but keep me solidly in the present as well. They allow me to become part of the shields, so I understand and remember their history, just as they surround and enter me and fill my one-room apartment with the presence of those for whom the shields are named. The spirits are living entities, evoking the world in which I lived for close to five years, giving life not only to the spirits of humans but to the spirits of the symbols carved and painted on the face of the shields—the flying foxes, the shell nosepieces that are wild boars, the heads of rayfish, the wriggling snakes, the curled tails of cuscus. When I open the door and enter, the spirits rush at me, invade my body like wondrous dybbuks wanting no exorcism but egging me on to write and put their voices onto paper.

Among the shields hang a variety of artifacts, from ancestor figures to spears, daggers for ritual killings, and necklaces of human vertebra, dog teeth, pig teeth, flying-fox teeth—objects from Asmat. There are also dozens of lime containers from the Trobriand Islands of Papua New Guinea and from the Lesser Sunda Islands of Indonesia, used to hold the burned and crushed shell or coral, chewed with betel nut and the flower or leaf of the pepper vine, that is a mild intoxicant known from India to the far eastern edges of Melanesia. Beware, though. Too much lime will badly burn the mouth of anyone not used to it. Next to the containers on my Italian bread bin, the *madia* in which dough was put to rise, is a rectangle of dark gray Styrofoam into which I have stuck the additional pieces of paraphernalia necessary to the chewing of betel nut, close to a hundred intricately carved lime sticks of wood, bone, and tortoise shell, as well as one with a plastic top made from the handle of an umbrella.

My jungle envelopes me: sixty-five pots of begonias, ti-palms, *Ficus,* corn plants, Christmas cacti, euphorbias, philodendra, night-blooming *Cereus,* bromeliads, an aurelia, a croton, spider plants, a snake plant, Norfolk Island pines, and some whose names are not yet known to me. Most of them cover my windows, filtering the sunlight, but there are more than enough clear areas to give a perfect view of the Hudson River below me, glistening in the sun, and New Jersey beyond it. The plants are sensitive, sometimes irascible, containing their own spirits. They know my touch, my watering, my voice, my music, the light clicking of my computer. They react angrily when I am away: they wilt, lean, fall over, some die; but they are alert to my return and fill the air with their scent and beauty. When I open the door and enter, I am again in Asmat, leaving the outside world behind. Perhaps it is the spirits who write my stories.